6th Knowledge Management and Intellectual Capital Excellence Awards 2020

An Anthology of Case Histories

Edited by Dan Remenyi

6th Knowledge Management and Intellectual Capital Excellence Awards 2020: An Anthology of Case Histories

Copyright © 2020 The authors

First published December 2020

All rights reserved. Except for the quotation of short passages for the purposes of critical review, no part of this publication may be reproduced in any material form (including photocopying or storing in any medium by electronic means and whether or not transiently or incidentally to some other use of this publication) without the written permission of the copyright holder except in accordance with the provisions of the Copyright Designs and Patents Act 1988, or under the terms of a licence issued by the Copyright Licensing Agency Ltd, Saffron House, 6-10 Kirby Street, London EC1N 8TS. Applications for the copyright holder's written permission to reproduce any part of this publication should be addressed to the publishers.

Disclaimer: While every effort has been made by the editor, authors and the publishers to ensure that all the material in this book is accurate and correct at the time of going to press, any error made by readers as a result of any of the material, formulae or other information in this book is the sole responsibility of the reader. Readers should be aware that the URLs quoted in the book may change or be damaged by malware between the time of publishing and accessing by readers.

Note to readers: Some papers have been written by authors who use the American form of spelling and some use the British. These two different approaches have been left unchanged.

ISBN: 978-1-912764-83-9

Published by: Academic Conferences International Limited, Reading, RG4 9SJ, United Kingdom, info@academic-conferences.org

Available from www.academic-bookshop.com

Table of Contents

Acknowledgements ii

Introduction iii

AI and Social Good in the Context of Sex Trafficking: Design Space and Best Practices 1

    Mayank Kejriwal

Strategic Responses to Disruptions: A Mobilization/ Response Plan to Manage Knowledge and Intellectual Capital in the Built Environment During Trying Times 11

    Ellyn A. Lester

The English Language School Case 23

    Göran Roos and Irina Gromova

Innovative Model for Development of Learning Organisations Through KM and Intellectual Capital 45

    Slavica Trajkovska, Angelina Taneva-Veshoska and Srecko Trajkovski

Acknowledgements

We would like to thank the judges, who initially read the abstracts of the case histories submitted to the competition and discussed these to select those to be submitted as full case histories. They subsequently evaluated the entries and made further selections to produce the finalists who are published in this book.

Dr G. Scott Erickson is Professor and Chair of Marketing in the School of Business at Ithaca College, Ithaca, NY, USA. He holds a PhD from Lehigh University, Masters degrees from Thunderbird and SMU, and a BA from Haverford College. His most recent book, New Methods in Marketing Research and Analysis was published by Edward Elgar in late 2017.

Dr Eduardo Tomé, gained his PhD in Economics in 2001, with a thesis on the European Social Fund. Since then he has worked in several Portuguese private universities. Since September 2013 he has worked at Universidade Europeia in Lisbon, Portugal. His main interests are Intangibles (Human Resources, Knowledge Management and Intellectual Capital), Social Policy and International Economics (globalization and the European Integration).

Francesca Dal Mas is a Lecturer in Strategy and Enterprise at the Lincoln International Business School in Lincoln, UK. She holds a PhD in Managerial and Actuarial Sciences and aMaster's Degree in Business Administration from Udine University, Italy and a Law Degree from Bologna University, Italy. Her research interests include strategy, knowledge management, and intellectual capital.

Introduction

2020 sees the sixth year of the Knowledge Management and Intellectual Capital Excellence Awards. This year we received 10 case histories for our consideration. After an initial evaluation of the abstracts and full review of those case histories which made it to the second round, we are pleased to present the four finalists in this anthology.

Each of these case histories demonstrate innovative and creative examples of knowledge management or intellectual capital implementation, covering a range of applications including AI and social good; Strategic responses to disruptions; Development of learning organisations and how IC can affect strategy implementation in a school setting. The case histories this year illustrate a diverse group of ideas from Russia, Macedonia and the USA.

The overall winner of the 2020 Knowledge Management and Intellectual Capital Awards will be announced at the end of the 21st European Conference on Knowledge Management, which is held this year as a virtual event, supported by Coventry University in the UK on 2-4 December 2020.

Dr Dan Remenyi
November 2020

iv

AI and Social Good in the Context of Sex Trafficking: Design Space and Best Practices

Mayank Kejriwal
Research Assistant Professor (Industrial and Systems Engineering) and Research Lead (Information Sciences Institute) at the University of Southern California, USA
kejriwal@isi.edu
Website: http://usc-isi-i2.github.io/kejriwal/

Abstract: Human trafficking (and especially, child sex trafficking) continues to be an urgent problem that affects developed and developing countries alike. The growth of the Web has made the problem much worse. According to a recent whitepaper at the UN Concordia Summit in New York City (September, 2019) that the author was involved in, there has been exponential growth in the volume of child pornography circulated online since the Web itself came of age in the late. However, the proliferation of illicit information on the Web presents a golden opportunity for investigators, policy makers and socio-economic stakeholders such as NGOs and scientists, to attack the problem from a data-driven perspective by applying Artificial Intelligence and knowledge management practices to the data. Such an application runs the gamut from applying appropriate data collection and cleaning methodologies to presenting explainable outputs to the stakeholders and incorporating their subsequent feedback into the pipeline. In our own work, we have designed a knowledge management and AI pipeline that has facilitated fruitful collaborations at an international level with social scientists from Nebraska, US federal law enforcement agencies, roundtable groups who feature leaders and investors from industry, and with a non-profit in India. In conjunction with other technologies, our pipeline has already led to prosecutions in human trafficking in the United States and has been used by over 200 law enforcement agencies. Today, we are also applying it specifically for finding victims of child sex trafficking from a corpus of advertisements on the Internet, and for conducting scientific analyses on the scope of the problem. In this case history, we will present architectural underpinnings and the design space of our pipeline, and also detail best practices and lessons learned along the way. Our hope is that this case history will provide guidance to data scientists and AI practitioners in applying their methodologies for social good, to assist those experts who are least versed in such advanced systems.

1. Introduction and Objectives

Web advertising related to Human Trafficking (HT) activity has been on the rise in recent years (Szekely et al. 2015). Question answering over crawled sex advertisements to assist investigators in the real world is an important social problem. This problem involves many technical challenges (Kejriwal & Szekely 2017a). This case study will describe a knowledge management solution to the problem of domain-specific search (DSS), a specific set of technologies that can address these challenges. Evidence from the HT domain shows that our solution has already provided valuable utility to analysts and investigative experts all over the United States.

In illicit domains such as HT but also others like securities fraud and narcotics, domain-specific search involves a form of Information Retrieval (IR) that takes as input a large domain-specific corpus of pages crawled from the Web. A good DSS engine allows investigators to satisfy their information needs by posing sophisticated queries to the engine using an intuitive format such as a Graphical User Interface (GUI), which is necessary since investigators are largely non-technical. A workflow of the process is described in the next section on Infrastructure. A fully functional DSS engine must have some notion of semantics, since sophisticated queries go beyond just keyword specification. This is because investigative queries are more like real-world questions requiring complex operations like aggregations (e.g., find me all email addresses linked to the phone 123-456).

Over years of careful research funded under the DARPA MEMEX[1] program, an architectural framework has been developed as an admissible and principled way of building an end-to-end DSS for illicit domains, with particular emphasis on human trafficking. One instantiation of the architectural solution, available as both open source code and executable in a stand-alone Docker container, is the domain-specific insight graph or DIG system that was built in our group at the University of Southern California's

---

[1] A general description of the MEMEX program can be accessed at https://www.darpa.mil/program/memex. Domain-specific search technology developed under MEMEX can be used for constructing and using DSS engines not just for illicit domains, but also non-illicit domains. Many of the tools have been released as open source under permissive licenses.

Information Sciences Institute. DIG was rigorously evaluated on real-world data collected from over 90,000 sex-advertising webpages collected over the first half of 2016 (Kejriwal, Szekely & Knoblock 2018). The principles behind DIG have been replicated independently by an industrial team. In conjunction with other technologies developed under DARPA MEMEX, DIG has been used to prosecute traffickers in the US, and to rescue trafficking victims. Recently, an engine of this type was being used by over 200 law enforcement officials to fight the overall problem of sex trafficking and related illicit activities. This case history details DIG, its design space, the lessons learned, impact and current development.

2. Infrastructure

An architectural overview of DIG is provided in Figure 1. As a first step, the system attempts to discover relevant websites in the user's *domain of intent* through a process that goes alternately by the name of *domain discovery* or *intelligent crawling*. In the literature, the latter term is more prevalent, having been researched under various settings (Aggarwal, Al-Garawi & Yu 2001), but more recently, the former term has also started becoming popular (Krishnamurthy, Pham, Santos & Freire 2016). The idea is to (iteratively) accept as input, various intuitive cues describing the domain such as keywords and websites, and find *relevant* webpages on the Open Web that seem to conform to the definition of the domain. For example, in the human trafficking domain, seed keywords would include terms such as 'escort' and 'massage parlor' and a seed website might be 'backpage.com'. Concerning relevance determinations, one could use classic techniques (such as a pre-trained learning-to-rank classifier) but over the course of the MEMEX program, methods employing reinforcement learning and lower-supervision machine learning paradigms have also been explored with success. A good example of a system implementing many of these techniques and also offering an intuitive interface to the user who is attempting to provide seeds and define the domain, is the open-source ACHE system, developed by a group at New York University (Krishnamurthy et al. 2016), and integrated into DIG.

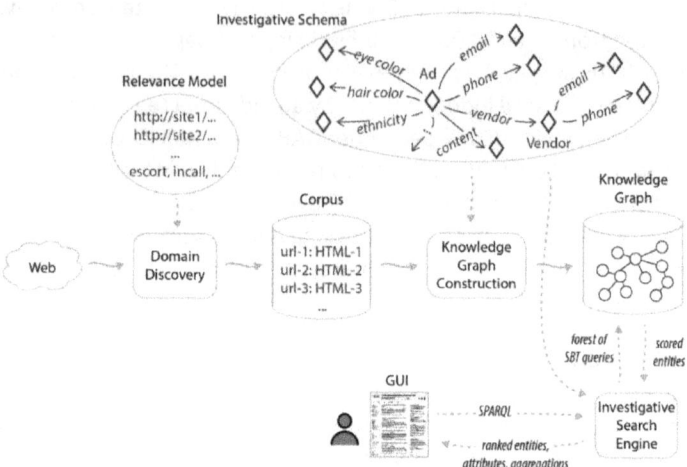

Figure 1: The key components in the Domain-specific Insights Graphs (DIG) workflow

The second step, which is much more challenging and can determine the quality (especially, precision) of the system and its outputs as a whole, is knowledge graph construction (KGC). KGC encompasses a set of roughly sequential techniques, such as information extraction, entity resolution and advanced knowledge graph identification methods such as knowledge graph embeddings (Kejriwal, 2019). All of these techniques are designed to operate in tandem to ingest a corpus of raw data (usually, natural language documents or 'semi-structured' webpages) as input and to output a knowledge graph (KG), which is defined as a directed, labeled multi-relational graph expressing entities (labeled nodes) and relationships between entities (labeled edges).

One aspect of an illicit domain DSS that should never be underestimated is the design of the Graphical User Interface (GUI) that the non-technical user uses to access the system. The backend of the system, including the actual query posed against a NoSQL database (Elasticsearch) used in DIG, should be insulated from such users. However, the user should still be given control both over KGC and over the search itself. Considerable research and user testing was conducted on systems like DIG to ensure that users were equipped to handle and remember system functionalities. In the case of KGC, users were shown how to define their investigative schema and declare meta-attributes like the importance of fields, whether the field should be visible to search against, the data type (e.g., numeric vs. string) of the field etc. Users were also able to handle expressive search facilities, including when to declare a specification as optional. A visualization of the GUI, used to investigate an actual human trafficking case (with key identifiers redacted), is shown in Figure 2.

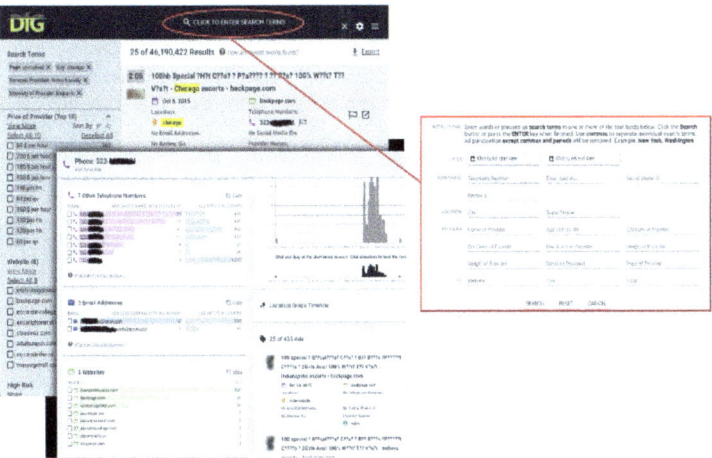

Figure 2: The main search page in DIG (underlaid) and an *entity* page (overlaid) describing a complete profile of a phone number, including co-occurrence with other phone numbers and email addresses, and the timestamps associated with ads from which that phone was extracted. Ads from which that phone were extracted are also suggested in the lower right pane. The search form is illustrated on the right.

3. Challenges

Building a DSS infrastructure that is generalizable and robust, and that will be accepted by law enforcement, involves several technical challenges that must be overcome, especially with limited resources. Table 1 briefly lists and describes some of these challenges. In normal cases, to maintain good quality and coverage, an investigative customer would have no choice but to hire a technical team to understand their needs and construct a DSS over months or years of effort. This is out of reach for resource-strapped investigative agencies in most countries. DIG manages to provide a solution in the design space that impacts law enforcements' operations in catching traffickers without requiring them to invest undue resources or place unwarranted trust in a technical system.

Table 1: A non-exhaustive set of challenges that an illicit-domain DSS must generally overcome to be useful to real-world investigators

Heterogeneity of webpage structure, making web information extraction systems difficult to automate with sufficient quality. In the human trafficking domain, many sex ad portals have to be crawled, which makes generalization and manual training too infeasible
Non-traditional nature of domain, including linguistic patterns (such as obfuscated language and use of emojis) and types of fields in the domain ontology; e.g., physical attributes, phones, locations and sex services provided have to be extracted for HT
Scale and infrastructure, since a truly comprehensive DSS must involve sophisticated query execution over domain-specific corpora crawled at Web-scale
Robustness to potentially irrelevant content both in the corpus and within webpages; for example, in the human trafficking domain, webpages on backpage.com and other portals often feature sponsored ads that can be difficult to automatically ignore
Presence of missing values and noise, due to both information obfuscation (see below) and due to imperfection in the AI systems for extracting key attributes; e.g., due to creative writing of phone numbers in the human trafficking domain, and conflation with other numeric attributes like age
Robustness to information obfuscation, since illicit players are often trying to evade investigative search by creatively masking identifying information so that automated systems would have a hard time extracting phone numbers, names and locations
Complex query types, since domain-specific search for investigative IR involves operations like aggregation and dossier generation, in addition to ordinary 'point-fact' style queries that are trying to search on a single piece of information
Preclusion of live Web search, due to the dynamic nature of illicit domains where webpages are frequently taken down and possibly 're-posted', sometimes with different pictures and locations. To answer questions involving time series, for example, pages have to be *cached*, which makes scale even more of a challenge. In the human trafficking domain, such pages have also been used for evidence gathering (as the MEMEX tools have been used in various documented prosecutions).

4. How the initiative was received by the users

Along with other tools in the DARPA MEMEX program, the DIG tool was permanently transitioned in late 2017 to over 200 law enforcement agencies (the primary users) in the United States. We note the following impacts:

- Our system ingested over 100 million+ sex advertisements from the Open Internet, providing over 3+ years of data coverage to law enforcement, and a total of 2 billion triples in the constructed knowledge graph;
- At least three known convictions of human traffickers have been publicly attributed to our systems (as well as to other MEMEX tools) by law enforcement, in addition to positive testimonials from the offices of multiple district attorneys in the US (San Francisco, New York);
- The tools show that victims are being victimized less, since prostitution arrests in New York have reduced by almost 3x since the tools were rolled out, while the fraction of arrest cases further investigated for abuse and human trafficking has gone from less than 1% (pre-toll rollout) to more than 62% when law enforcement last reported the results;
- Finally, we have given demonstrations and tutorials on the tool at multiple academic and industrial venues over the last three years, and actively collaborated with multiple stakeholders, including social scientists. There has also been some ongoing work to extend the scope of the tool to illicit domains beyond human trafficking, including illegal weapons sales, mail shipment fraud and penny stock fraud.

5. Learning outcomes

The case study described herein was developed over many years of research, and many valuable learning outcomes have emerged as a consequence. Below, we describe some of the primary lessons learned:

- Automatic, high-quality data acquisition is the new bottleneck in AI-driven systems. Many, if not most, of our users expressed satisfaction with the facilities offered by DIG and felt that the potential of DIG would have been more fully realized if the quality of the data ingested had been better. Unfortunately, we had no control over this issue, although the DARPA MEMEX program used state-of-the-art data acquisition, relevance modeling, and crawling systems. One area of future work currently being considered is the integration of domain discovery and knowledge discovery. While such an integration would introduce new complexities and dependencies into the system, it could potentially improve data acquisition quality by incorporating richer user feedback into the domain discovery process.

- Users should be empowered to dynamically specify their own vocabularies and ontologies using trial-and-error. In the AI literature, there are powerful data models and representations for specifying fine-grained ontologies. These have merits in certain fields, such as biomedicine, but are not suitable for users who do not explicitly deal with vocabularies, ontologies, or data models on a regular basis. Instead, systems like DIG allow users to crystallize their internal vocabularies by exploring the data and specifying fields as they go along; for example, many of our users added new concepts to the domain ontology while they were building the relevance model in the domain discovery model, step-by-step. This methodology is in sharp contrast to the more traditional view of specifying a domain model upfront before data acquisition, processing, or modeling begins.

- Provenance, going all the way to the original source, is key to fostering trust among (particularly, non-technical) users. We are, by no means, the first to make this observation, but believe that it is important to (re-)state owing to the rapid progress in deep learning technologies for information extraction, without the same progress in interpreting or explaining the results. Users expressed trust in our system because of the provenance offered both at the web page and extraction levels. We note that, recently, the AI community has recognized this issue and is tackling the explainability problem with vigor. In our own work, we proposed techniques inspired by network science to automatically assess the noise in information extraction outputs (e.g., phone number extractions from webpages) without any kind of manual annotations (Kejriwal & Kapoor 2019). In the future, this work could be used to build customized search engines and systems that are 'recall-friendly' (contain more relevant information, but also more noise), 'precision-friendly' (contain less, but more accurate, information) or otherwise capture some user-specified tradeoff.

Perhaps the biggest lesson of all is that any such technology, to have large-scale and impact-driven deployment, must have a holistic, interdisciplinary focus i.e. all stakeholders, and especially the users, must be actively involved in the design process, and the development of the technology itself must be assumed to be necessarily non-linear. There are going to be false starts and false assumptions, but only through experience, patience and trial-and-error can a truly novel system be developed to tackle a social problem of this magnitude. We are optimistic about the future, and believe that this case study is just one instance in a series of potential applications seeking to apply 'knowledge graphs' and AI for social good (Kejriwal & Szekely 2017b).

6. Plans to further develop the initiative

The initiative is already being developed in active collaboration with federal agencies in the United States to focus specifically on detecting international sex trafficking, including cases of smuggling and child sex trafficking. In addition to improving the algorithms and workflow, we describe two lines of work where our future efforts are focused:

- We are extending our workflow with algorithms and tools to provide leads to law enforcement on children who are currently missing or being trafficked. Active investigations are now open because of the work we are doing, and we have initiated communications with other organizations in this space to collaboratively address this problem using a greater variety of data. We are also developing minimally supervised 'indicator mining' tools that automatically mine indicators (such as for drug use activity, movement across cities, and so on) that are known to be correlated with trafficking activity (Kejriwal et al. 2017).
- While our focus has always been on assisting law enforcement and other agencies in rescuing and rehabilitating human trafficking victims, an equally important agenda is to investigate the data using scientific methods, both to understand the landscape and social structure of the online sex industry (without being subject to bias or unsubstantiated theory), as well as drive data-driven policy debate and recommendations. In 2019, we have already done a first such

study (to the best of our knowledge, the only such study) using the entirety of UK sex ads and metadata (Kejriwal & Gu 2020). Currently a US-wide study is underway.

References

Aggarwal, C.C., Al-Garawi, F. and Yu, P.S., 2001, April. Intelligent crawling on the World Wide Web with arbitrary predicates. In *Proceedings of the 10th international conference on World Wide Web* (pp. 96-105).

Kejriwal, M., Ding, J., Shao, R., Kumar, A. and Szekely, P., 2017. Flagit: A system for minimally supervised human trafficking indicator mining. *arXiv preprint arXiv:1712.03086*.

Kejriwal, M. and Kapoor, R., 2019. Network-theoretic information extraction quality assessment in the human trafficking domain. *Applied Network Science*, 4(1), p.44.

Kejriwal, M. and Gu, Y., 2020. Network-theoretic modeling of complex activity using UK online sex advertisements. *Applied Network Science*, 5(1), pp.1-23.

Kejriwal, M., Szekely, P. and Knoblock, C., 2018. Investigative knowledge discovery for combating illicit activities. *IEEE Intelligent Systems*.

Kejriwal, M. and Szekely, P., 2017a, October. An investigative search engine for the human trafficking domain. In *International Semantic Web Conference* (pp. 247-262). Springer, Cham.

Kejriwal, M. and Szekely, P., 2017b. Knowledge graphs for social good: an entity-centric search engine for the human trafficking domain. *IEEE Transactions on Big Data*.

Krishnamurthy, Y., Pham, K., Santos, A. and Freire, J., 2016. Interactive exploration for domain discovery on the web. *Proc. of KDD IDEA*.

Szekely, P., Knoblock, C.A., Slepicka, J., Philpot, A., Singh, A., Yin, C., Kapoor, D., Natarajan, P., Marcu, D., Knight, K. and Stallard, D., 2015, October. Building and using a knowledge graph to combat human trafficking. In *International Semantic Web Conference* (pp. 205-221). Springer, Cham.

Author Biography

Dr. Mayank Kejriwal is a Research Assistant Professor and Research Lead at the University of Southern California. His research is in applied AI for solving human-centric problems such as human trafficking and crisis response. He is the author of an upcoming textbook on knowledge graphs (MIT Press, 2021).

Strategic Responses to Disruptions:
A mobilization/ response plan to manage knowledge and intellectual capital in the built environment during trying times

Ellyn A. Lester
Stevens Institute of Technology, New Jersey, USA
elester@stevens.edu

Abstract: At Stevens Institute of Technology, CM 530 Strategic Responses to Cyclical Environments tackles the strategic planning process and its usefulness to architecture, engineering, and construction firms. Critical success factors like competitive intelligence and knowledge management are explored. In Spring 2020, the evolving COVID-19 Pandemic was integrated into an assignment on Mobilization and Response Plans. During this timeframe, New York City had its first positive case, which exploded into more than 1,000 active cases, greatly affecting the students' plans. The assignment fulfilled multiple course learning outcomes. After the assignment was submitted, the class continued with COVID-19 as the primary experiential case study. In the future, the Pandemic will be used as a case study to address strategic planning based on documented and timely real-world events. Additionally, a mixed methods research study will document how leaders in New York's Built Environment responded to this global challenge.

1. Introduction

As an elective course focused on the Built Environment at Stevens Institute of Technology, CM 530 *Strategic Responses to Cyclical Environments* develops an understanding of the strategic planning process and its place in successfully guiding architecture, engineering, and construction (A/E/C) firms to continued superior performance. As such, competitive intelligence and knowledge management are key elements that are fused into each component of the course to emphasize their place as critical factors that affect every organization's ability to maintain competitive advantage.

This is defined in the first sentence of the course description, which states that successful professionals "must consider masses of ambiguous information, yet forge meaningful plans for the future," and concludes by stating that successful executives need "a combination of tough analytical thinking, strategic planning skills, intuition, grit, and a little bit of luck."

All of these attributes were necessary during the Spring 2020 semester as COVID-19 ravaged New York City and the tri-state (New York, New Jersey and Connecticut) area. Of course, none of this was obvious when the course began the last week of January. On January 17th, the first COVID-19 cases were confirmed in Washington State and Illinois, the former more than 3,000 miles away and the later just over 800 miles away. It wasn't until March 1st that the first case was detected in New York City (Axelson, 2020).

By March 11th, New Jersey reported its first death (Porter, 2020) less than 10 miles from the Stevens' campus; as a result, New York's Governor Andrew Cuomo declared a State of Emergency (Axelson, 2020). Stevens Institute mandated that all on-ground, face-to-face courses transition to online learning (Stevens, 2020). By the end of the semester in early May, more than 350,000 New York residents would be COVID-19 positive with more than 22,000 fatalities (New York State Department of Health, 2020) and more than 145,000 residents of New Jersey would be COVID-19 positive with more than 10,000 fatalities, (State of New Jersey Department of Health, 2020) with the United States at almost 1.5 million positive cases and almost 90,000 deaths, representing more than 30% of the total cases reported worldwide (Johns Hopkins University of Medicine, 2020).

As an experientially-focused course based on Kolb's Learning Theory adding "real world" experience to theoretical knowledge (Raelin, 1997), e.g. Porter's strategic planning theories, while drawing from Nonaka and Takeuchi's concept of *explicit vs tacit knowledge* and adding Raelin's *work-based learning models*, the course uses *case-based learning* to integrate theory and practice. This requires a dynamic interplay between the individual and the collective, e.g. class group work that progressed from finding common ground by defining terms and reading classic management and strategic planning theories, to deliberately questioning those theories in practice based on their own experiences, while reflecting on the tacit knowledge shared by experienced professionals and determining whether it supported the theories introduced throughout the course.

In the best case, as a course progresses the group becomes a *community of practice* thinking and acting in collaboration and enjoying a common language and history. Unfortunately, this best-case scenario was challenged when COVID-19 became a global epidemic, and New York City and its immediate surroundings became the epicenter. As the course then shifted to online learning, all students and faculty found themselves in unpresented circumstances, including "stay-at-home orders," enforced curfews, mandatory use of masks and social distancing, and forced closure of all non-essential businesses with associated record-high unemployment creating lines at food banks, supply chain disruptions, and mental health issues amongst residents, (Choi, 2020; Mutikani, 2020; Panchal, 2020).

In alignment with the foundations of the course, and in an attempt to help the students persevere during the crisis, the instructor incorporated the pandemic into each assignment, providing opportunities to question assumptions, think critically, change approaches with agility, and function during uncertain times.

One case study focused on creating a proactive, responsive *COVID-19Mobilization/Response Plan* for their previously assigned firms. The key objectives of the assignment were to provide critical information to firm constituents, to minimize disruption to business processes, and to alleviate constituents' concerns due to the ongoing uncertainty resulting from the pandemic.

Table 1.1: COVID-19 Mobilization/Response Plan Assignment

Covid-19 Mobilization/Response Plan
Assigned: March 02, 2020 **Due:** March 16, 2020 **Portion of Grade:** (200 points) As the Chief Knowledge Officer (CKO) you are responsible for creating Mobilization/Response Plan including the following sections: <ul><li>Risk Assessment Analysis</li><li>Crisis Communication</li><li>Incident Management</li><li>Resource Management</li><li>Business Continuity</li><li>Implementation</li></ul>You are responsible for disseminating the plan, as necessary, so that everyone affiliated with the organization understands that:<ul><li>change must occur,</li><li>what will be implemented,<ul><li>and how these changes will help make the organization successful.</li></ul></li></ul>

The evolving nature of the pandemic meant that students had to be flexible and timely in their responses, updating the *Mobilization/Response Plan* several times over the course of the two-week period. At the start of the assignment, New York had its first positive case; by the due date, there were 950 cases in New York State, precipitating the closing of public schools, bars, movie theaters, gyms, and restaurants (Axelson, 2020). This greatly affected the students' plans as well as the information disseminated to their constituents. Nonetheless, the students were eager and fully engaged in the assignment, asking questions, sending out memos, and actively debating the efficacy of proposed actions.

Ellyn A. Lester

> March 12, 2020
> Dear XXXXXX Staff,
> We are open and will remain open for business. As concerns for the staff's health and wellness increase due to the potential risk of exposure to COVID-19, XXXXXX will enact the following policies:
> CoVid-19 Action Plan:
> - We urge any staff member to stay at home at the first sign of COVID-19 like symptoms and to continue to stay home until those symptoms have dissipated. Extended paid sick time will be allowed and will **not** be deducted from your yearly sick time bank.
> - If you are affected by school closures, you will be permitted to work from home.
> - Staff members directly exposed to COVID-19, but asymptomatic, must telecommute.
> - Should a staff member test positive, we will advise staff immediately and implement working from home under self-isolation throughout the virus's two week incubation period.
> - XXXXXX will provide deep cleaning and sanitizing of the office before staff return.
> - Requests for remote working options must be approved prior to implementation.
> - For payroll and timekeeping purposes, notify your Managing Principal if you are ill, believe you have been exposed to the virus, or are working remotely per the above policies.
> - Whenever a teleconference can be utilized, staff members should recommend that and facilitate.
> - Zoom meetings are encouraged for all meetings.
> - Business related travel options will be considered on a case by case basis by the Managing Principal.
> - Offsite staff will work within the conditions dictated by their client at that location.
>
> While the COVID-19 Action Plan is in effect, the following remote working policy will be in place:
> - Communication updates will be transmitted via XXXXXX.com email etc.
> - Staff working remotely must be available during normal business hours. Staff will not be required to read or respond to emails outside of normal business hours.
> - <u>Remote access set-up must be completed no later than Monday, March 15 by 7:30 am.</u>
> - <u>Zoom and Slack set-up must be completed no later than Monday, March 15 by 7:30 am.</u>
>
> Important Reminders: Follow CDC & Health Official's recommendations which include:
> - Clean hands with hand sanitizer or wash hands with soap/water for 20 seconds.
> - Cover your face with your arm/elbow when coughing or sneezing.
> - Do not touch your face.
> - Perform routine cleaning of your personal workspace (alcohol wipes will be provided).

Figure 1.1: Firm Internal Memo: COVID-19 Crisis Communication (May 12, 2020)

XXXXXX COVID-19 Action Plan Update
To be implemented starting Tuesday March 17, 2020

Operations
• Project Manager and Staff will work remotely unless otherwise required, with Principal approval.

• When office attendance is required, if non-public transportation is utilized, it will be reimbursed.

• Administration will provide continuous in-office presence 5 days a week on a rotational basis.

• Principals will provide continuous in-office presence 5 days a week on a rotational basis.

• Most project business will be conducted remotely using tools outlined in the COVID-19 Action Plan.

• As an additional tool, project teams may elect to utilize MS Teams Application with Principal Approval.

Timecard procedures for remote operations
• All timecards are to be completed by Thursday COB including projects for the coming Friday.

• Timecards are to be submitted and printed as a PDF document.

• The Timecard pdf will be loaded into folders residing in the Library Server.

• Timecards shall use the following naming convention: 2020-03-20 Last Name_First Name.pdf

• Each staff member will contact their PM to notify them that their timecard has been submitted.

• Project Managers will review timecards. Upon approval, PMs will insert their initials into the file name.

• As each timecard is approved, the last approving PM will move the timecard to the "Approved" folder.

Expense Report procedures for remote operations
• All Expense Reports are submitted on a bi-weekly basis in conjunction with the payroll period.

• Expense Reports will be submitted and printed as a PDF document with receipts then forwarded to the PIC.

• Principals will approve each Expense Report and forward it to Accounting.

• Accounting will mail checks to staff members.

Figure 1.2: Firm Internal Memo: COVID-19 Crisis Communication (May 17, 2020)

After the assignment was complete, the class continued to monitor the epidemic, utilizing it as an ongoing case study throughout the semester. It is intended that this assignment will be used in future semesters to demonstrate the strategic planning process, focusing on the tenets of competitive intelligence and knowledge management while immersing theory into a timely, relatable real-world event.

2. The infrastructure required to launch the initiative

When a completely new virus was discovered only weeks before the course started in January 2020, no one could have predicted that the United States would face so many challenges. Thus, everyone had to be continuously flexible and timely in their responses, and open minded about the many new initiatives that became necessary from hour to hour and day to day.

Even though most students were familiar with CANVAS, the online learning platform, new software such as Zoom, Microsoft Teams, etc. had to be implemented on the fly. Even so, with increased effort the transition to online learning was successful.

3. The challenges encountered

Several key challenges had to be overcome to make the course successful. While the most critical was the continuously evolving nature of the pandemic, moving the course from on-ground to online in 24-hours was challenging for the instructor; presentations and classroom introductions had to be conducted via Zoom, all discussions and assignments had to be created in CANVAS and theoretical explanations had to become extremely detailed. It was also difficult for the students; they had to spend many hours in Zoom meetings, complete numerous small assignments that would typically have been *in-class* activities and maintain positive mindsets despite extreme isolation.

Each of these was overcome through perseverance. While not mandated by the institution, the instructor elected to lead weekly live Zoom meetings. At the beginning and end of each class, the instructor conducted a "check in" with the students and reminded them that they could reach out anytime. Cell phone numbers were exchanged by anyone willing to share, including the instructor's personal cell number.

4. How the Initiative was Received

Students were interested and invested in the assignments, particularly those who had internships. The instructor encouraged students to discuss the assignments with their supervisors and to share their submissions if the supervisor requested.

A few students provided unsolicited feedback, "... coupling the strategic planning process with a real external threat like COVID-19 was very intriguing and helpful in understanding the impact of COVID-19 on the construction industry, construction personnel and the economy. In addition to the impacts, analyzing and preparing a course of action, to minimize the economic and health suffering due to COVID-19 was also in complete harmony to the topics we studied during the course. Overall, it was a great learning experience."

Another student focused more on their personal experience, "I truly enjoyed this semester with you, although this is a tough year for all of us. Thanks for your company this semester, it was not easy for me to get through it because I got my undergraduate degree and spent four years in Wuhan. I know how dangerous the virus is and I definitely have no capacity to face it while in US. Meanwhile, I cannot go home because the airline banned travel into China, although I do understand it. So, your caring words really encouraged me and made me feel better. I know that maybe none of us say a word about this in class, but I am sure that it works."

5. Learning Outcomes

Many of the Course Learning Outcomes were fulfilled by the COVID-19 Mobilization/Response Plan assignment. After the assignment was complete, the students demonstrated an ability to:

- Practice the use of established strategic planning techniques within the context of the "Built Environment"
- Analyze disruptive professional issues and initiatives as both threats and opportunities within Construction Management
- Identify and distinguish alternative approaches for managing their position from a Construction Manager's perspective, as well as their own, during volatile business cycles

- Demonstrate effective career planning in all stages of the Built Environment's cyclical business environment when faced with imperfect or insufficient information

Utilizing a rubric, the instructor evaluated each student's performance on the assignment and assessed their mastery of the activities listed in the Course Learning Outcomes (CLOs). Each student did well on the assignment, and all met the requirements of the CLOs.

6. Plans for Further Development

While the students were completing the COVID-19 Mobilization/Response Plan, it became clear that the pandemic was becoming a global phenomenon. Thus, the instructor integrated aspects of the epidemic into each of the remaining assignments. Each student was asked to continue monitoring their assigned organization and upload any documents that indicated how the organization was managing the outbreak. During weekly Zoom sessions, they were encouraged to discuss any actions their firms were taking and evaluate such initiatives potential for success.

The instructor also used the pandemic as an example when presenting theories, concepts, etc. It became an ongoing case study integrating theoretical concepts such as intellectual capital, knowledge management, and strategic planning, as well as change management initiatives, with *real world disruptions* that have a direct effect on an organization's success and ability to maintain long-term competitive advantage.

Utilizing the materials purposively collected throughout semester, including firm announcements, podcasts and webinars from *communities of practice*, and articles collected in industry publications, the instructor will work with a select group of volunteer students to conduct a mixed method study to determine COVID-19's impact on the A/E/C industry in New York City. In turn, this research will provide professional guidance to the industry as it navigates the "new normal," post-pandemic business landscape.

References

Axelson, B. (2020). 'Coronavirus timeline in NY: Here's how Gov. Cuomo has responded to COVID-19 pandemic since January,' *Advance Local Media*, 15 April [Online]. Available at: https://www.syracuse.com/coronavirus/2020/04/coronavirus-timeline-in-ny-heres-how-gov-cuomo-has-responded-to-covid-19-pandemic-since-january.html (Accessed: 06 May).

Choi, T.Y., Rogers, D., Vakil, B. (2020). Coronavirus is a wake-up call for supply chain management. *Harvard Business Review*, 27 March [Online]. Available at: https://hbr.org/2020/03/coronavirus-is-a-wake-up-call-for-supply-chain-management. (Accessed: 14 April).

John Hopkins University of Medicine Coronavirus Resource Center. (2020). *Covid-19 Dashboard by the Center for Systems Science and Engineering (CSSE) at Johns Hopkins University (JHU)* [Online]. Available at: https://coronavirus.jhu.edu/map.html (Accessed: 14 May).

Kolb, D. A., J. S. Osland and I. M. Rubin (1995), *Organizational Behavior: An Experiential Approach*, Englewood Cliffs, N.J.: Prentice-Hall.

Mutikani, L. (2020). Coronavirus: over 20 million Americans have now applied for unemployment benefit, *World Economic Forum*, 16 April [Online]. Available at: https://www.weforum.org/agenda/2020/04/united-states-unemployment-claimants-coronavirus-covid19 (Accessed: 20 April).

New York Department of Health. (2020). *Persons tested positive by county*, 14 May [Online]. Available at: https://covid19tracker.health.ny.gov/views/NYS-COVID19-Tracker/NYSDOHCOVID-19Tracker-Map?%3Aembed=yes&%3Atoolbar=no&%3Atabs=n (Accessed: 16 May).

Nonaka, I. & Takeuchi, H. (1995). *The knowledge-creating company: How Japanese companies create the dynamics of innovation*, New York: Oxford University Press.

Panchal, N. Kamal, R., Orgera, K., Cox, C. Garfield, R. Hamel, L., Munana, C. and Chidambaram, P. (2020). The implications of Covid-19 for mental health and substance abuse,' *Kaiser Family Foundation*, 21 April [Online]. Available at: https://www.kff.org/coronavirus-covid-19/issue-brief/the-implications-of-covid-19-for-mental-health-and-substance-use/ (Accessed: 01 May).

Porter, D. (2020). '1st COVID-19 death in New Jersey was veteran horseman,' *AP News*, 11 March [online]. Available at: https://apnews.com/8ae6fdfa2fdf6c87ab6608e109453b51 (Accessed: 12 March).

Realin, J.A. (1997). A model of work-based learning. *Organization Science*, 8(6), 563-578.

State of New Jersey Department of Health. (2020). 5/12/20. *New Jersey COVID-19 dashboard* [Online]. Available at: https://www.nj.gov/health/cd/topics/covid2019_dashboard.shtml (Accessed: 12 May).

Stevens Institute of Technology. (2020). 3/9/20: *Health advisory #10: plans to move classes online and additional new guidance* [Online]. Available at: https://www.stevens.edu/directory/student-health-services/health-advisory-update/coronavirus-2019-covid-19-information/advisories-updates/march-2020 (Accessed: 01 May).

Author Biography

Ellyn Lester, PhDc is the Director of Built Environment Programs and Associate Chair of Graduate Studies for the CEOE Department at Stevens Institute of Technology. Her research focuses on "Knowledge Sharing through Mentorship in the Built Environment" as part of the larger arena of "Gaining Competitive Advantage in Project-Based, Cyclical Environments.

The English Language School Case

Göran Roos[1] and Irina Gromova[2]
[1]Institute of Economics and Management, Immanuel Kant Baltic Federal University, Kaliningrad, Russian Federation
[2]English School №1, Kaliningrad, Russian Federation
goran@roos.org.uk
exaggeration@bk.ru

1. Introduction

One of the questions facing boards and management around strategy implementation, defined as converting a strategy into action by the people in the organisation (Hacker et al, 2001; Mintzberg, 1994), is: Are we implementing this strategy in the most optimal way possible to maximise the creation of value (however value is defined). The literature is generally weak as relates to both how overall strategy implementation should take place and on how optimality in speed and effectiveness can be achieved and evaluated (Mintzberg, 1994; Kaplan, 1995; Noble, 1999a; Hitt et al., 2017). Saunders et al. (2007) reported that as relates to strategy implementation there was neither any benchmark studies nor any dynamic models found in the literature (this is still true in the more recent literature review by Siddique & Shadbolt, 2016 and). There are some, but not many, models of strategy implementation taking the managerial perspective on the process e.g. Collins & Huge (1993), Hacker & Akinyele (1998), Noble (1999b), Hacker et al. (2001), Hrebiniak (2005), Saunders (2005), Hrebiniak (2013), and it would also be possible to include the somewhat simplistic Brightline (2017) in this list.

According to The Economist Intelligence Unit (2017) 61% of organisations struggle with bridging the gap between strategy formulation and implementation and 53% stated that ineffective strategic initiatives negatively impacts the organisation's performance and competitive advantages. The lack in strategy implementation capability results in not achieving the expected results from the strategies developed. A 2004 survey by Marakon Associates and the Economist Intelligence Unit showed that firms achieved only 63% of the expected results and the analysis further indicate that this gap is mainly due to failure in implementing the strategy effectively (Mankins & Steele, 2005).

In order to implement a strategy, managers must actively manage the firms resource portfolio in terms of which resources to acquire and develop and which to divest and abandon as well as how the resources in the portfolio are going to be deployed (Sirmon et al., 2007). In a continuously changing competitive landscape this resource configuration must be continuously adapted to stay effective (Fernström & Roos, 2003; Yi et al., 2016; Roos, 2018).

If the organisation is applying any of the resource based view, the dynamic capability view and the competence-based view (see Roos, 2019, for a detailed discussion) the lack of managerial guidance provided by the toolboxes associated with these strategic views presents a challenge for strategy implementation (Sanchez, 2008; Lockett et al., 2009; Kraaijenbrink et al., 2010; El Shafeey & Trott, 2014).

The purpose of this initiative is to illustrate how an IC based operationalisation of the resource based view of the firm (RBV) can provide insight from a resource portfolio perspective around how a strategy has been implemented and how this implementation can be improved. The setting for the initiative is English School #1by Irina Gromova which appeared on the educational map of Kaliningrad region (Russia) in September 2012. It grew out of a small group of 6 students aged 8-16 in one20 square meter classroom, and two creative teaches who aimed at both receiving and providing premium level knowledge of English, literature, history, science and maths. From the first day of its existence the school set itself up as a high-quality educational establishment with the corresponding requirements on both teaching staff and students. The knowledge and the level of English their students reached was supported by the internationally recognised Cambridge Certificate (levels a1-c2).

The two founders and co-owners did not initially possess much knowledge of running any form of business. Like many entrepreneurs they worked on an intuitive basis, using common sense and the impeccable reputation of one of the co-owners as an English teacher with 20 years' experience. This approach enabled the organisation to, over five years, successfully grow into a serious educational establishment with solid reputation, 900 students aged 6-58 and 15 designer classrooms in prestigious premises of 400 square meters in the business centre of the city. When Irina Gromova as a co-owner shifted her role from being a teacher to taking on the fulltime responsibility as CEO, the company started to more formally develop its resource portfolio, with an emphasis on human, relational and organisational resources, with the aim of continuously providing offerings that exceeds the quality required by the upper end of the market.

Within a few years the range of educational products was extended to also include adult education and continuous professional development courses for English teachers. The articulated strategic intent of the organisation is *"to provide premium class, high quality education, and to become a solid platform for its students to enter the social and professional elite"*. The corresponding company values were identified, articulated and embraced as: perfection, uniqueness, depth, leadership, motivation, interaction, traditions & innovations, and versatility.

The organisation has 15 teachers - established professionals in the field considering their age. Among them there are 6 with bachelor's degrees, 7 with master's degrees and 2 with PhD's in linguistics. All teachers hold C1/C2 certificates holders – the highest levels of proficiency and mastery in their command of the language. All teachers are also frequent participants in different English language teaching methodology and linguistics conferences.

The school have well-articulated and implemented standards and procedures for the learning process. These are supported by a strong corporate culture built over the period five-year period. An important part of this culture is the ethics relating to all communications with participants and stakeholders. A stakeholder is a party that has an interest in a company and can either affect or be affected by the business and in this case they include but are not limited to employees, students, parents, certifying and quality controlling organisations, government entities, landlords, suppliers, etc.. They are prioritised based on the work of Agle et al. (1999), using the dimensions of power, legitimacy and urgency into prioritised stakeholder groups under the headings of Definitive, Dominant, Dependent, Dangerous, Dormant, Discretionary and Demanding (see Figure 1).

Legitimacy is a generalised perception or assumption that the actions of an entity are desirable, proper or appropriate within some socially constructed system of norms, values, beliefs and definitions from the viewpoint of the majority of stakeholders. Urgency is the degree to which a stakeholder claims call for immediate attention. A stakeholder group has an urgent interest when its needs are of a time-sensitive nature and when they are important or critical to its mission. Power is the probability that an individual or group within a relationship is in a position to carry out its own will despite resistance, bearing in mind that powerful stakeholders may be able to exert influence that will affect a project either negatively or positively. Power is the ability to control what decisions are made and to facilitate the implementation of these decisions. Power may be coercive, based on the use of force or the threat of force; utilitarian, relying on material persuasion or incentives; or normative, involving more symbolic influence.

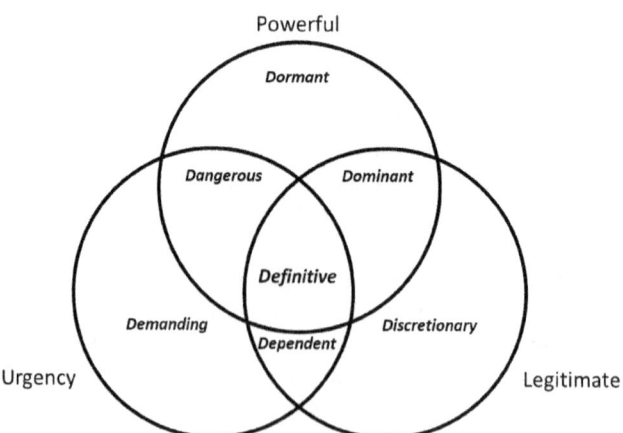

Figure 1: The Stakeholder Classification Framework (after Agle et al., 1999)

The positioning of any given stakeholder is dynamic and can change almost instantly as events occur and contexts change. The primary focus of the organisation are the definitive stakeholders (Students, Teachers, Parents, Certifying and quality controlling agencies) and then dormant (e.g. government agencies) and discretionary (e.g. suppliers) stakeholders.

With time the above-mentioned values and the strategy of differentiation gave rise to premium-class programs for personal and professional development alongside with the standard ones aimed solely at language learning. The programs now concentrated on developing soft-skills including: Life Strategy, Time-Management, Getting Things Done, Self-Marketing, Emotional Intelligence, Critical Thinking and Leadership programs. Such shift from solely language teaching to a focus on personality development required a 'fresh look' at arranging and using company resources. This 'fresh look' was taken using the IC Navigator approach with the intent of identifying improvement opportunities in the, de-facto, RBV grounded strategy in use.

2. The infrastructure

The process around the 'fresh look' involved workshops, direct discussions with the CEO and peer discussions between the school's CEO and other CEOs in non-educational businesses.

The process of the workshops involved the identification of the firm's resources and the classification of these into the different categories (See Table 1 for the resource taxonomy).

This is to be done to at least level three in the Resource Distinction Tree (the level below the five overarching resource types). The resulting distinction tree as identified by management is shown in Figure 2. Each of the resources shown are defined and understood by the management team in an explicit way. Some of these definitions are shown in Table 2.

Table 1: Resource Taxonomy and characteristics[1]

	Monetary Resources	Physical Resources	Intellectual capital category		Human Resources
			Relational Resources	Organisational Resources	
Description	Financial resources that take the form of cash assets (such as marketable securities) that can easily be converted to pure cash	Anything that can be touched, for example has a physical presence (that is what you would normally find under the heading of plant and equipment in the balance sheet)	The relationships held by individuals on behalf of the firm or that are embodied in the form of contracts with the firm as one party. The outcome of desires to hold explicit or implicit relationships with the firm by external parties	The result of human endeavours developed internally in the firm or acquired externally by the firm that is now owned by the firm and that are not physical or monetary in nature	All useful resources that are embodied in people
Owned and Controlled by	Firm	Firm	Nobody owns, and the resource is co-controlled	Firm	Individual
Economic behaviour	Decreasing marginal return	Decreasing marginal return	Network economic behaviour	Network economic behaviour	Increasing marginal return
Known conversion rate to monetary value	Yes	No	No	No	No
Additive	Yes	Yes	No	No	No
Information asymmetry	Low	Low	High	High	High
Rivalry Resource	Yes	Yes	No	No	No
Excludability	Yes	Yes	No	Partial	No
Examples of appropriation mechanisms[1]	Financing structure and cost of capital	IP Firm specific assets	First mover advantage Network size Reputation Bargaining power Customer retention	Causal ambiguity Contracts Agreement stability Imperfect mobility Brand	Shared Values/Goals Innovativeness Absorptive capacity
Drives towards a strategic logic (in the meaning of Stabell & Fjeldstad, 1998) of:	Value Chain	Value Chain	Value Network Although can drive towards a value shop logic in the very early stages of the resource lifecycle and towards value chain in the very late stages of the resource lifecycle	Value Network Although can drive towards a value shop logic in the very early stages of the resource lifecycle and towards value chain in the very late stages of the resource lifecycle	Value Shop

---

[1] "value appropriation mechanisms do not create new value but instead determine the relative share of relational rents that the focal firm can appropriate" (Lavie, 2007, p.1191)

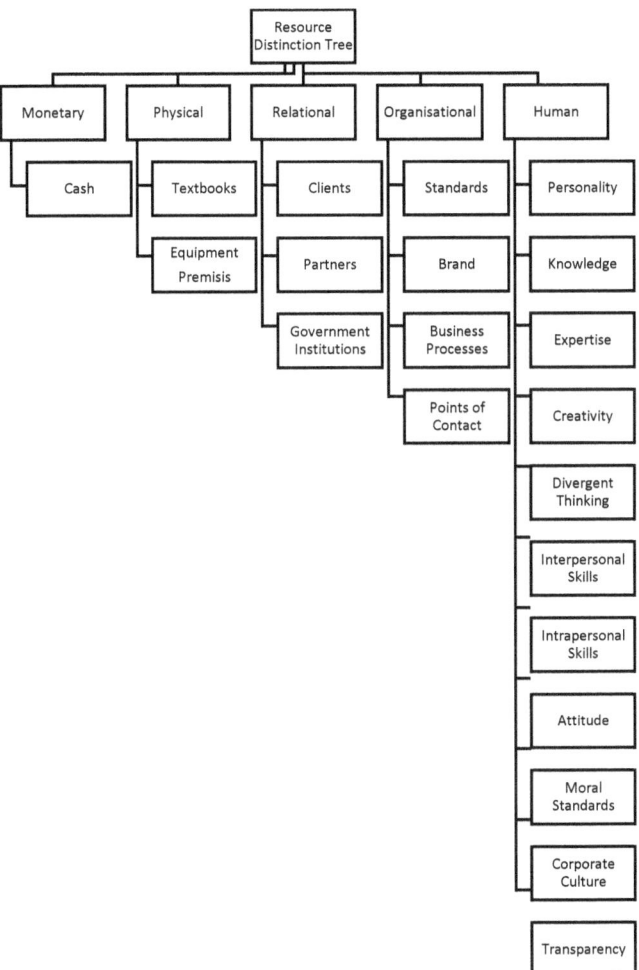

Figure 2: Resource Distinction Tree for the Case Organisation using the labels of the CEO

Table 2: Definition of the non-intuitive resource categories

Resource	Definition
Points of Contact	
Personality	Include warmth, cognitive organisation, orderliness, indirectness, and problem-solving ability.
Knowledge	Professional knowledge which is a function on the subject taught or the administrative job executed
Expertise	Subject matter expertise and classroom management skills (including ability to communicate awareness of student behaviour; the ability to attend to more than one issue at once; smoothness and momentum as relates to the transition through different activities; keeping children attending to activities and with the group; monitoring and maintenance of student performance; a balanced ratio of motivating comments to the total number of transitions; the degree to which varied activities are given during a defined time block).
Creativity	Openness, levels of ideation, autonomy, expertise, exploratory behaviour.
Divergent Thinking	Nonconformity; curiosity; willingness to take risks; persistence; physical, social and cognitive spontaneity; manifest joy; sense of humour.
Interpersonal Skills	Active listening, Teamwork, Responsibility, Dependability, Leadership, Motivation, Flexibility, Patience, Empathy
Intrapersonal Skills	Self-esteem, open mindedness, being aware of your own thinking, ability to learn, understand and manage your own emotions, self-confidence, self-discipline, self-motivation, overcoming boredom, being patient, self-starter, take initiative, working independently, being persistent, having a positive attitude, and being a good manager of time.
Attitude	The organisation's agreed and expected way of thinking or feeling about our educational business. This is then reflected in the behaviours of the organisational members (teachers and administrative staff). This attitudes encompass but are not limited to: a favourable and optimistic view of students and their potential; embracing evidence based new pedagogical insights and new technological tools that support learning; a willingness and ability to adapt one's teaching to meet the individual educational needs of students; continuously striving for self-improvement. The social and emotional attitudes a teacher holds support positive teacher-student relationships and effective classroom environments.

Resource	Definition
Points of Contact	
Moral Standard	The norms which we have in our organisation about the types of actions which we believe to be morally acceptable and morally unacceptable. Specifically, we focus on matters which can either seriously harm or seriously benefit our students.
Corporate Culture	The beliefs and behaviours that determine how our employees and management interact with each other and with external stakeholders. Our corporate culture is only partly defined in an explicit way since it dynamically develops over time based on the (changing) people that are part of the organisation. The primary carrier of and norm for the corporate culture is Irina Gromova.
Transparency	The openness, communication, and accountability that exists in the organisation's relationship to its students their parents and other stakeholders.

Weighting the resources according to their influence on value creation in the organisation. This is done by distributing 100 points across all the possible transformations in that matrix row. This fixed-sum allocation approach is aimed at capturing latent or unobserved utility (Carson et al., 1994). Alternative approaches in (Louviere, 1994) include: (1) ranking alternatives in order of preference; (2) series of paired comparisons; (3) picking best and worst alternative; (4) bundle selection by choosing a given number of best alternatives; (5) consider/not consider in making decision; (6) judgmental ratings, for achieving the same objective, have not worked equally well when tried in executive MBA settings in the early phases of developing the IC Navigator approach (Roos, 2019). This fixed-sum allocation is done by asking the question: "How relatively influential is this transformation when it comes to contributing to the organisation's value creation?" It is not about how large the transformation is; it is about how much it matters. This is an important distinction since small transformations may matter a lot whereas large transformations may not matter a great deal. To improve the precision of this step the following process is used: (1) each individual in the team documents their own answer to the question; (2) for each resource in the resource ranking process or for each transformation in the transformation influence ranking the team member with the highest and lowest point allocation is identified; (3) these two individuals put forward their respective arguments for why they have allocated this high or low amount of points; (4) a group discussion follows where these arguments are debated and a consensus reached on the allocation to be given to this resource or transformation.[2] In addition to increasing the precision in the data capture this process also deepens the management team's common understanding of what goes on in the firm's resource portfolio. The result of this step is a matrix where every row adds up to 100 and where each transformation that has been assigned a weight greater than zero is defined; this means that the question: 'what do we mean by this transformation?' is answered. The result of this process is depicted in the form of a Normalised Resource Transformation Matrix were transformations are from the row headings to the column headings and the resource weightings (out of one hundred) are found in the rightmost Σ headed column (the transformation matrix for the case firm is shown in Figure 3).

Resource category	Resource weight	Resource	Cash	Textbooks	Equipment	Premises	Clients	Partners	Government Institution	Standards	Brand	Business Processes	Points of Contacts	Personality	Knowledge	Expertise	Creativity	Divergent Thinking	Interpersonal Skills	Intrapersonal Skills	Attitude	Moral Standards	Corporate Culture	Transparency	Σ
Financial 5 %	5%	Cash	0.00	0.00	0.15	0.00	0.00	0.15	0.00	0.15	0.50	0.50	0.60	0.15	0.65	0.70	0.15	0.15	0.10	0.00	0.90	0.10	0.05	0.00	5
Physical 5 %	5%	Textbooks	0.36	0.00	0.06	0.00	0.45	0.15	0.09	0.09	0.06	0.06	0.21	0.09	0.24	0.33	0.24	0.09	0.09	0.09	0.06	0.06	0.15	0.06	3
	1%	Equipment	0.00	0.01	0.05	0.03	0.10	0.01	0.00	0.10	0.05	0.10	0.10	0.00	0.10	0.07	0.06	0.07	0.00	0.00	0.05	0.00	0.10	0.00	1
	1%	Premises	0.00	0.03	0.00	0.01	0.05	0.05	0.00	0.03	0.20	0.05	0.20	0.10	0.00	0.00	0.03	0.05	0.00	0.03	0.10	0.01	0.06	0.00	1
Relational 41 %	21%	Clients	3.15	0.00	0.63	0.00	2.31	0.42	0.42	0.63	0.63	0.42	0.42	1.47	1.47	0.63	1.47	0.84	1.47	0.63	1.47	1.47	0.42	0.63	21
	10%	Partners	0.50	0.20	0.50	0.00	1.50	0.50	0.80	0.50	0.30	0.50	0.60	0.00	0.70	0.80	0.40	0.10	0.60	0.50	0.30	0.30	0.10	0.30	10
	10%	Government Institution	1.00	0.00	0.40	0.00	0.50	0.50	0.50	0.70	1.00	0.70	0.50	0.00	0.90	0.90	0.00	0.40	0.90	0.20	0.50	0.20	0.00	0.20	10
Organisational 20 %	10%	Standards	0.80	0.30	0.70	0.30	0.80	0.80	0.50	0.30	0.80	1.00	0.80	0.30	0.30	0.30	0.00	0.20	0.40	0.30	0.50	0.10	0.40	0.10	10
	5%	Brand	0.90	0.20	0.15	0.05	1.00	0.25	0.25	0.15	0.10	0.20	0.30	0.20	0.00	0.10	0.30	0.10	0.20	0.10	0.25	0.05	0.15	0.00	5
	3%	Business Processes	0.24	0.00	0.24	0.30	0.36	0.15	0.09	0.30	0.09	0.09	0.27	0.18	0.00	0.06	0.00	0.03	0.06	0.03	0.09	0.12	0.24	0.06	3
	2%	Points of Contacts	0.20	0.04	0.10	0.06	0.40	0.14	0.14	0.04	0.20	0.06	0.04	0.06	0.00	0.00	0.06	0.10	0.06	0.04	0.06	0.06	0.12	0.02	2
Human 29 %	4%	Personality	0.60	0.08	0.20	0.04	0.64	0.28	0.28	0.12	0.32	0.12	0.20	0.12	0.12	0.12	0.20	0.08	0.04	0.04	0.12	0.12	0.12	0.04	4
	5%	Knowledge	0.70	0.05	0.40	0.05	0.45	0.40	0.40	0.25	0.60	0.20	0.15	0.10	0.10	0.15	0.20	0.10	0.10	0.10	0.15	0.10	0.20	0.05	5
	5%	Expertise	0.70	0.05	0.40	0.05	0.45	0.40	0.40	0.25	0.60	0.20	0.15	0.10	0.15	0.20	0.10	0.10	0.10	0.15	0.10	0.20	0.05		5
	3%	Creativity	0.30	0.12	0.30	0.03	0.39	0.15	0.15	0.21	0.30	0.00	0.18	0.15	0.06	0.06	0.06	0.09	0.09	0.12	0.03	0.09	0.03		3
	2%	Divergent Thinking	0.20	0.08	0.20	0.02	0.26	0.10	0.10	0.14	0.20	0.00	0.12	0.10	0.04	0.04	0.04	0.06	0.06	0.08	0.02	0.06	0.02		2
	2%	Interpersonal Skills	0.22	0.00	0.00	0.00	0.24	0.18	0.18	0.00	0.24	0.06	0.06	0.08	0.08	0.10	0.08	0.04	0.08	0.06	0.08	0.10	0.04		2
	1%	Intrapersonal Skills	0.00	0.00	0.05	0.00	0.09	0.08	0.08	0.00	0.10	0.00	0.05	0.08	0.05	0.05	0.02	0.05	0.03	0.01	0.07	0.07	0.10	0.02	1
	2%	Attitude	0.16	0.06	0.08	0.06	0.24	0.14	0.14	0.06	0.22	0.06	0.06	0.08	0.08	0.08	0.06	0.06	0.06	0.06	0.04	0.06	0.10	0.04	2
	2%	Moral Standards	0.00	0.00	0.00	0.00	0.24	0.24	0.00	0.20	0.20	0.14	0.00	0.22	0.00	0.00	0.05	0.00	0.14	0.16	0.16	0.10	0.14	0.00	2
	2%	Corporate Culture	0.12	0.06	0.08	0.04	0.16	0.06	0.06	0.08	0.16	0.10	0.04	0.20	0.08	0.08	0.06	0.04	0.08	0.10	0.16	0.12	0.08	0.04	2
	1%	Transparency	0.00	0.00	0.02	0.00	0.14	0.09	0.09	0.04	0.13	0.04	0.05	0.06	0.00	0.00	0.00	0.00	0.04	0.04	0.06	0.06	0.07	0.07	1
	100%	Σ																							100

Figure 3: Normalised Resource Transformation Matrix for the case firm (most influential transformation in bold)

---

[2] Herein lies a potential weakness in the approach since it may well be the individual with the, in the setting and context, most persuasive debating style or the individual with the highest hierarchical position in the debating group who wins the argument rather than the individual with the deepest knowledge or strongest argument in terms of causality logic. This is a phase in the *IC Navigator* process where the facilitator needs to pay specific attention so that the risk for these outcomes are minimised.

Evaluation of the contribution to value creation provided by each of the identified resources is done using an effector plot (this is a plot of the resource importance on the x-axis versus the logarithm base 10 of the quote between the effort that comes out of a resource divided by the effort that goes into that same resource on the y-axis. Complementing this visual categorisation, two additional delineator curves can be constructed in the effector plot. The delineator curves are calculated for the logarithmic plot as the functions for which the least square line of best fit and the y-axis are asymptotes. These functions are oblique, meaning that the numerator of the function has a degree exactly one greater than the denominator and this is exemplified in the expression of the function f(x):

$$f(x) = \frac{x^2 + ax + b}{cx + d}$$

In the case of the logarithmic effector plot the least square line of best fit will have the form y= ax+b which is one of the asymptotes and the other is the line x=0. In this case the above simplifies into the asymptotes (A) being $A(x) = ax + b \pm \frac{c}{x}$, where a is the slope of the least square line of best fit and b is the intercept of the least square line of best fit) This is shown in the upper part of Figure 4. Visualisation is the best way to facilitate the path from data to knowledge whilst imposing the minimum load on both cognitive abilities and short-term memory. This is used to depict the IC Navigator generated from the Matrix. The convention places the organisational resource in the middle of the visualisation, the monetary resource at the top left, the physical resource at the top right, the relational at the bottom right, and the human at the bottom left. Standardising layout as well as the colours used for the different resource categories allows for faster and more intuitive insights when visualisations of different transformation matrices are put side by side. The circles represent the resource importance, and the arrows represent the transformation importance. The resulting depiction is shown in the middle of Figure 4. Finally, the behaviour of the resources that underpin the firm's value creating activities will determine the behaviour of the firm. These behaviours are generally called strategic logics and are summarised in Table 3 and further elaborated in Table 4. It is possible to conclude that the more even the balance between the three strategic logics in a given organisation, the more challenging for management to achieve a good value creating outcome; and the more uneven the balance, the easier it is for management to achieve a good value creating outcome. This is because the logics are to some extent contradictory in their optimisation requirements e.g. focus on achieving benefits from economies of scale for value chains, from economies of scope for value shops, and from network economics for value networks. This follows from the behaviour of the resources that underpin these logics. It is possible to illustrate the level of managerial challenge by illustrating the balance between these strategic logics as deduced from the importance of the resources to the observed organisation. This can be done using a ternary plot where the most challenging position from a managerial point of view is at the centre of the plot and the least challenging position is at any of the three corners of the plot (see the ternary plot for the case organisation in the bottom of Figure 4).

Table 3: Brief overview of the three strategic logics (extracted from Roos et al., 2005, table 1.2, p. 23-26)

Attribute	Type of Strategic Logic (Value chain named by Porter (1985) and Value Shops and Value Networks named by Stabell & Fjeldstad, 1998)		
	Value Chain	Value Shop	Value Network
Original designation by Thompson (1967)	Long-linked technology	Intensive problem-solving technology	Mediating and facilitating technology
Business problem	Transforming inputs to outputs	Mobilising resources and structure activities to solve unique customer problems	Linking willing participants across time and space to enable direct and indirect exchanges
Business Focus	Product or Service	Solutions to problems (enabling shift from one state to a more desirable state)	Connections
Competitive Focus	Scale, Capacity utilisation	Scope, Personnel utilisation	Coverage, Network utilisation
Value creation process is	Sequential	Cyclical and iterative	Simultaneous and parallel

Attribute	Type of Strategic Logic (Value chain named by Porter (1985) and Value Shops and Value Networks named by Stabell & Fjeldstad, 1998)		
	Value Chain	Value Shop	Value Network
Value creation Logic	Understood by disaggregating the value creation process of the firm into discrete activities that contribute to the firm's relative cost position and create a basis for differentiation. Disaggregation must be complete in the sense that it captures all the activities performed by the firm	Understood by recognising that the flow of activities is not linear but iterative between activities and cyclical across the activity set resulting in a high degree of both sequential and reciprocal interdependence between activities often involving multiple disciplines and specialities in spiralling activity sets (where each cycle implements the solution to the problem that follows from the solution implemented in the previous cycle)	Understood by recognising that a concurrent and layered set of activities is required to service efficiently a random need for mediation services between many customers
Inherent organisational focus	Efficiency	Effectiveness	Neither Efficiency nor Effectiveness
Underpinned by resource categories	Monetary Physical Organisational (in the last phase of the resource life cycle) Relational (in the last phase of the resource life cycle)	Human Organisational (in the first phase of the resource life cycle) Relational (in the first phase of the resource life cycle)	Organisational (in intermediate phases - almost all - of the resource life cycle) Relational (in intermediate phases - almost all - of the resource life cycle)

Table 4: Some exhibited characteristics of value chains, value shops and value networks (extracted from Roos et al., 2005, p. 28-29)

For **value chains**—a world dominated by monetary and physical resources—characteristics that will be exhibited will include:	For **value shops**—a world dominated by human resources—characteristics that will be exhibited include:	For **value networks**—a world dominated by relational and organisational resources—characteristics that will be exhibited include:
• Secrecy being paramount (since a small advantage will be rapidly caught up by competition) • Size mattering, and a push for monopoly inherent in the activities of the organisation (since it is a world dominated by economies of scale) • Standardisation, leading to a push attitude toward customers (since it is a world dominated by economies arising from experience and learning, requiring repetition and thereby standardisation) • Relative certainty about short-term future value that can be realised from these resources. • Relative ease with which market prices are established for these resources.	• Openness, dialogue, and discourse being paramount (since a small advantage rapidly grows into a large advantage). • Larger size not necessarily being better, and market share not necessarily being relevant, both rather being seen as irrelevant or being rapidly overturned (since it is a world dominated by economies of scope). • Standardisation being counterproductive, indeed there being a drive to solve the same problem differently the second time around to maximise learning, leading to a pull attitude toward customers (since it is a world dominated by economies of scope). • Relative uncertainty about short-term future value that can be realised from these resources. • Relative difficulty, perhaps impossibility, in establishing universal and verifiable market prices for these resources.	• Cooperative efforts such as agreeing on standards and joint marketing having appeal (since in the early phase of building a resource, cumulative investments will have small returns). Once the marginal return on investment passes a certain level and continues to increase, a sharing of insights will become common. Once the resource enters the area of decreasing marginal returns, organisational behaviour will take on the characteristics of value chains and operate much more as though in the world dominated by monetary and physical resources. • Size matters, but here the optimal market share is not 100 per cent but rather the point at which maximum marginal return is to be expected since it is a world dominated by network economics. • Management of the different phases being paramount, leading to challenges around the phase changes since it is a world dominated by network economics. • Relative uncertainty about short term future value that can be realised from these resources. • Relative difficulty in establishing universal and verifiable market prices for these resources.

The workshops were complemented with discussions with the CEO all of which resulted in the output shown in Figure 4.

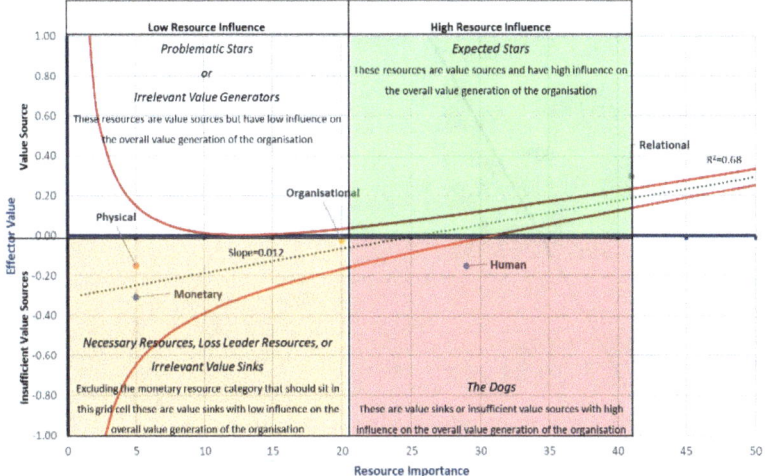

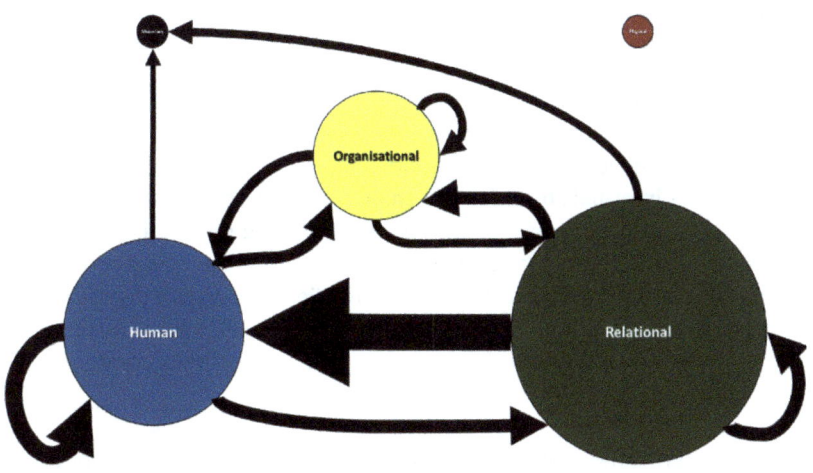

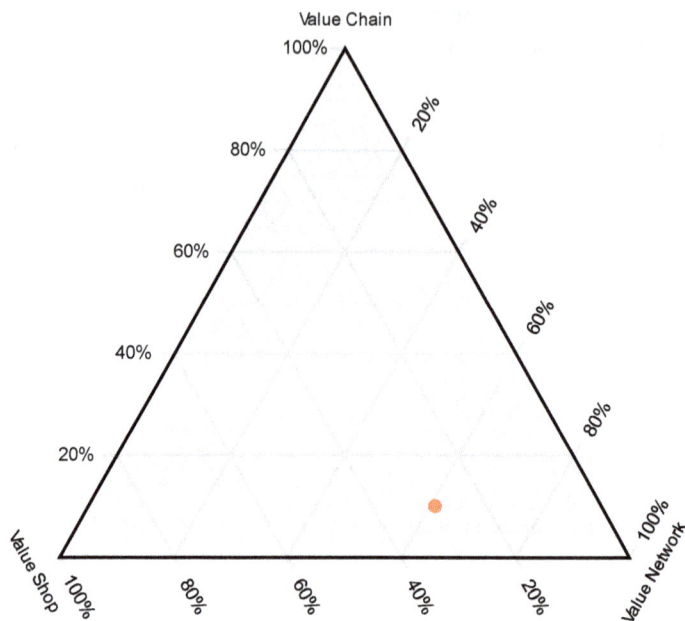

Figure 4: Effector plot, IC Navigator visualisation and ternary plot of the strategic logic positioning for the case company

3. The challenges

The challenge prompting the 'fresh look' were a combination of continued growth and a move into digital teaching. The growth challenge would put a strain on the informal structure of a small organisation and require a higher degree of formalisation as well as reemphasising the relative importance of some resources. The digital challenge is similar to those other educational institutions face in moving to on-line and mobile delivery with the associated necessary changes in how value is created (see Roos, 2018 for a discussion of digital transformation and EF Hello [https://www.efhello.com/] for an example).

In process terms the challenge was primarily around the development of the resource distinction tree and extracting the CEO's unarticulated value creation path. The first-time managers are required to identify, label and categorise resources (under the four constraints given on page 162 in Roos, 2019) can be challenging, and is best done in a facilitated discussion process. The knowledge required to do this does, however, reside within the combined heads of the senior management team although it may not previously have been expressed in this way. Care must be taken to ensure that the resource distinction tree that forms the starting point for the matrix is perceived to reflect accurately management's perception of reality. The detailed methodological considerations are outlined in Roos (2019).

4. How the initiative was received

The CEO valued both the process and the outcome of the process highly. The insights were implemented in the organisation and there were a high level of acceptance and support of all identified changes except for on-line learning among all definitive stakeholders albeit that the certifying and quality controlling agencies supported also the move to on-line learning. The move to incorporate on-line learning into the schools delivery met with resistance from teachers, students and their parents and the normal processes to manage change (first achieve understanding for why it is both necessary and good and secondly get acceptance and support from those impacted)[3]. The dormant stakeholders expressed no view on the changes that followed from the process and did not request any further information after being informed. Likewise, the discretionary stakeholders only reacted based on self-interest e.g. suppliers of the on-line related equipment and supply reacted positively whereas suppliers of equipment and supply that is substituted reacted negatively.

5. The learning outcomes

The initial effector plot was optimised using the Frontline Solver software with the boundary conditions (hundreds) and constraints (hundreds) were agreed with the CEO and some also involved a facilitated peer-to-peer discussion with other CEOs from non-educational businesses. The evaluation and optimisation principles are based on Roos (2019, pp. 216-226). This

---

[3] It is worth noting that with the outbreak of the COVID 19 pandemic this initial resistance has been reversed to an almost admiration and total support for what is now perceived to be insightful foresight by the CEO.

resulted in the effector plot of the proposed future value creation looking as depicted in Figure 5.

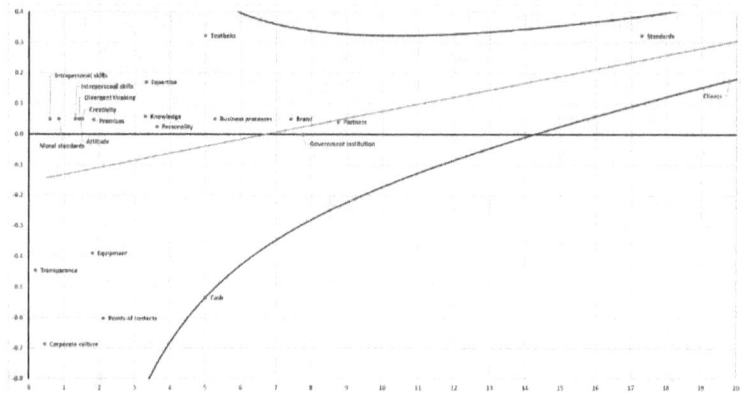

Figure 5: Optimised effector plot

Progressing through this process provided the management team at the School with a common language around strategy and resources as well as a common understanding of the key drivers of value and the value creation process. It did not take long to explain to the employees of the company the specifications and the nuances of the above-mentioned process and the strategy since every idea of the managerial team is always the subject of discussion among all company staff. Such sessions with employees did help to get a few important insights concerning the resources as well. There were two insights which were so powerful that they came to modify the focus and implementation of the strategy. The first was the crucial importance of relational resources and consequently some of the business processes relating to this resource group were modified, some transformed, others fine-tuned.

The fundamental philosophy of building the knowledge and competence of every member of the teaching team as thoroughly as possible did not change – it was still seen as the key to achieving the strategic intent. But rather than focusing on building the knowledge of the different individuals (human resource), the company changed the emphasis to putting mechanisms in place to extract the experience and tacit knowledge of the employees and turn it into an organisational resource. In this way the organisation can better leverage the knowledge of the individual: people can learn from other's experiences, they can pick up a project where somebody else has left it, and new employees can get up to speed more rapidly. It also reduces the risk associated with staff leaving and taking all valuable knowledge with them.

The second influential insight for the team was the understanding of transformations between resources and the realisation that they are the key to value creation. It is not primarily the stock of knowledge residing among the individuals in the organisation that would achieve superior shareholder value growth for the English School, but how they as an organisation were able to transform that knowledge into a process, a product, good reputation or something else that creates value – a value that will directly or subsequently be translated into financial returns for the owners.

These insights drove the School to become a process driven, learning organisation and in developing its on-line business. In practice this meant putting processes in place for supporting the teachers in creating new knowledge, but also on enshrining the knowledge in processes, structures and systems. Although many knowledge building initiatives had already been instigated in the spirit of bridging the previously defined competence gap, the IC Navigator process helped the management team focus, coordinate and integrate the initiatives into the streamlined value creation process to ensure a conscious building of the critical parts of structural resources.

Thus, the school is expecting to have 1000 students in the academic year 2020-2021 partly due to the changes instigated through the above outlined process.

6. Plans to further develop the initiative

The initiative is planned to be repeated to separate the school's businesses into two separate businesses from a value creating point of view including optimisation of the two separate business models: the on-line business and the face-to-face business. This will enable the value creation optimisation of each of these businesses and grounded in this the way they are structured into the one business is expected to be improved to maximise both overall value creation and inter-business synergies.

With the outbreak of the COVID 19 pandemic these plans have accelerated for the on-line business and been put on hold (due to lock-down) for the face-to-face business. Exactly how this will develop once the pandemic is over is as yet unclear.

References

Agle, B. R., Mitchell, R. K., & Sonnenfeld, J. A. (1999). Who matters to CEOs? An investigation of stakeholder attributes and salience, corporate performance, and CEO values. *Academy of management journal*, 42(5), 507-525.

Brightline, (2017). *Brightline 10 guiding principles*. Brightline Project Management Institute. Newtown Square, PA.

Carson, R. T., Louviere, J. J., Anderson, D. A., Arabie, P., Bunch, D. S., Hensher, D. A., Johnson, R. M., Kuhfeld, W. F., Steinberg, D., Swait, J., & Timmermans, H. (1994). Experimental analysis of choice. *Marketing Letters*, 5(4), 351-367.

Collins, B., & Huge, E. (1993). *Management By Policy: How Companies Focus Their Total Quality Efforts to Achieve Competitive Advantage*, ASQC Quality Press, Milwaukee, WI.

El Shafeey, T. & Trott, P. (2014). Resource-based competition: three schools of thought and thirteen criticisms. *European Business Review*, 26(2), 122-148.

Fernström, L. & Roos, G. (2003). Differences in Value Creating Logics and their Managerial Consequences. *International Journal of the Book*, 1.

Hacker, M. E., Kotnour, T. & Mallak, L. A. (2001). Formalizing deployment processes in the US Government. *International Journal of Public Sector Management*, 14(3), pp.221-240.

Hacker, M., & Akinyele, A. (1998). What happens after the strategic planning session is just as important as what happens during it. *National Productivity Review*, 17(4), pp.45-52.

Hacker, M.E., Kotnour, T. and Mallak, L.A., 2001. Formalizing deployment processes in the US Government. *International Journal of Public Sector Management*, 14(3), pp.221-240.

Hitt, M.A., Jackson, S.E., Carmona, S., Bierman, L., Shalley, C.E. and Wright, M., (Eds.), 2017. *The Oxford Handbook of Strategy Implementation*. Oxford University Press, New York, NY.

Hrebiniak L. G. (2005). *Making strategy work. Leading effective execution and change*, Pearson Education, Upper Saddle River, NJ.

Hrebiniak, L. G. (2013). *Making strategy work: Leading effective execution and change*. 2nd ed. FT Press, Upper Saddle River, NJ.

Johansson, E., & Svensson, J. (2017). *Implementing strategy? Don't forget the middle managers: Strategy implementation from a middle management perspective*. Masters Thesis. Institutionen för ekonomi, teknik och samhälle, Luleå tekniska universitet. Luleå, Sweden.

Kaplan, R.S., 1995. New roles for management accountants. *Journal of Cost Management*, 9(3), pp.6-13.

Kraaijenbrink, J., Spender, J. C. & Groen, A. J. (2010). The resource-based view: a review and assessment of its critiques. *Journal of management*, 36(1), 349-372.

Lavie, D. (2007). Alliance portfolios and firm performance: A study of value creation and appropriation in the US software industry. *Strategic Management Journal*, 28(12), 1187-1212.

Lockett, A., Thompson, S. & Morgenstern, U. (2009). The development of the resource-based view of the firm: A critical appraisal. *International journal of management reviews*, 11(1), pp.9-28.
Louviere, J. L. (1994). Conjoint Analysis. In R. Bagozzi (Ed.), *Advanced methods of marketing research* (pp. 223-259). Cambridge, MA: Blackwell Business.
Mankins, M. C. & Steele, R. (2005). Turning great strategy into great performance. *Harvard business review*, 83(7/8), p..64-72.
Mintzberg, H., 1994. *The rise and fall of strategic planning*, Prentice Hall, Hemel Hempstead, UK.
Noble, C. H. (1999b). Building the strategy implementation network. *Business Horizons*, 42(6), pp.19-19.
Noble, C.H., 1999a. The eclectic roots of strategy implementation research. *Journal of business research*, 45(2), pp.119-134.
Porter, M. E. (1985). *Competitive Advantage*. New York, NY: The Free Press.
Roos, G. (2018). Resource deployment system implications of migrating the firm into a digital value creation paradigm. *Knowledge Management Research & Practice*, 16(3), pp.281-291.
Roos, G. (2019). *Optimising resource deployment within the firm: overcoming theoretical problems with a practical application*, Doctoral Dissertation, University of South Australia, Adelaide, Australia.
Roos, G., Pike, S., & Fernström, L. (2005). *Managing Intellectual Capital in Practice*. Oxford, UK: Butterworth-Heinemann.
Sanchez, R. (2008). A scientific critique of the resource-base view (RBV) in strategy theory, with competence-based remedies for the RBV's conceptual deficiencies and logic problems, in Sanchez, M. (Ed.), *Research in Competence-Based Management, Vol 4 - A Focused Issue on Fundamental Issues in Competence Theory Development*, Emerald Group Publishing, Binley, UK, 3-78.
Saunders, A. M. (2005). *Performance excellence and strategy deployment: a framework for implementing strategic initiatives*, Doctoral dissertation, Massey University, Palmerston North, New Zealand.
Saunders, M., Mann, R. and Smith, R., 2007. Benchmarking strategy deployment practices. *Benchmarking: An International Journal*, 14(5), pp.609-623.
Siddique, M. I. & Shadbolt, N. M. (2016). *Strategy implementation literature review*. A report for DairyNZ AgriOne, Centre of Excellence in Farm Business Management.
Sirmon, D. G., Hitt, M. A. & Ireland, R. D. (2007). Managing firm resources in dynamic environments to create value: Looking inside the black box. *Academy of management review*, 32(1), pp.273-292.
Stabell, C. B., & Fjeldstad, Ø. D. (1998). Configuring value for competitive advantage: On chains, shops and networks. *Strategic Management Journal*, 19(5), 413–437.
The Economist Intelligence Unit. (2017). *Closing the Gap: Designing and Delivering a Strategy that Works*, Brightline Initiative, Project Management Institute. Newtown Square, PA.
Yi, Y., Li, Y., Hitt, M. A., Liu, Y. & Wei, Z. (2016). The influence of resource bundling on the speed of strategic change: Moderating effects of relational capital. *Asia Pacific Journal of Management*, 33(2), pp.435-467.

Author biographies

Göran Roos is a Visiting Professor at the Australian Industrial Transformation Institute, Flinders University, Adelaide; a Stretton Fellow appointed by the City of Playford at University of Adelaide; Adjunct Professor at the Institute of Economics and Management, Immanuel Kant Baltic Federal University, Kaliningrad. He is a member of several corporate and advisory boards. Göran is a fellow of both the Australian Academy of Technological Sciences and Engineering (ATSE) and the Royal Swedish Academy of Engineering Sciences (IVA).

Irina Gromova is Associate professor at the Institute of Linguistics at Immanuel Kant Baltic Federal University and owner and CEO of English School 1/Английская Школа 1 Ирины Громовой. She is a prominent Russian entrepreneur, a living legend of teaching and methodology in Russia

Innovative Model for Development of Learning Organisations Through KM and Intellectual Capital

Slavica Trajkovska[1], Angelina Taneva-Veshoska[1] and Srecko Trajkovski[3]
[1]Institute for Research in Environment, Civil Engineering and Energy, N. Macedonia
[2]Civil Engineering Institute Macedonia, JSC Skopje, N. Macedonia
slavica.trajkovska@iege.edu.mk ; angelina@iege.edu.mk
srecko.trajkovski@gim.mk

Abstract: This case serves as proof and inspiration for companies in developing countries, providing evidence of the positive effects on sustainable performance from managing intellectual capital (IC) and knowledge. In order to set the scene it should be noted that N. Macedonia is modest innovator, where business investments in R&D&I barely exist. The Civil Engineering Institute Macedonia (CEIM) has 45 years of experience in the construction industry in the Western Balkan region. The decision in 2014 to transform the company from a traditional to a learning organisation, was based on the assessed needs and life cycle stage, as well as the challenges of the environment (political and economic) and the vision for the future. All activities are implemented in accordance with CEIM Strategies: Development strategy, Strategy for human resources management and Strategy for KM. In 2014 CEIM established a private research institute (IECE), creating a collaborative innovation partnership. This approach has been recognized by WEF, emphasizing the collaboration between young and established companies that share resources and combine efforts to support innovative ideas. CEIM and IECE developed the CO-IN model as a holistic approach in university-industry collaboration in developing countries. Between 2014-2019 several strategic decisions, innovative actions, structural measures, and organisational changes have been developed and implemented based on the adopted strategies for investment and development of the human capital in CEIM. The results from the qualitative and quantitative analysis (Scandia Navigator, VAIC, cost-benefit, correlation) confirm the positive effects KM and IC have on the company's performance. The benefits that occurred due to the transformation are examined in detail and results show that this process of KM and IC is enhancing the competitiveness of the company and will bring even greater results in the long term.

1. Introduction

The initiatives for investments in knowledge, R&D&I, especially for the business sector barely exist. N. Macedonia spends only 0.22% of its GDP on R&D which is one of the lowest percentages in Europe (where the government is the biggest contributor to total R&D expenditures). Latest data shows that investments are 0.1.euro per inhabitant (EpI) in 2017 and 0.3 EpI in 2018, in comparison to EU in 2017 is 20.9 EpI.[1]

One of the few private companies that invest in knowledge, R&D&I in N. Macedonia is the Civil Engineering Institute MACEDONIA JSC SKOPJE (CEIM).

CEIM is a private company established in 1975 in Skopje, N. Macedonia, active in the construction industry. CEIM offers services in all areas of construction: planning, research, design, quality control, surveillance and construction. CEIM operates on the market in N. Macedonia, and through its subsidiaries regionally in: Serbia, B&H, Montenegro and Kosovo.

In a period of 5 years the Civil Engineering Institute MACEDONIA JSC SKOPJE (CEIM)[2] successfully transformed itself into a learning organisation, by setting up system for KM and IC. This is a very unique and rare case happening in N. Macedonia, a developing country and a modest innovator[3].

The CEIM strategy is designed with an orientation towards sustainable development and knowledge-based economy, improving the R&D activities and gain applied knowledge and competencies. The decision in 2014 to transform the company from a traditional organisation to a learning organisation, which learns and manages its knowledge and IC was initiated by the Supervisory Board of CEIM.

The need for implementing all the KM/IC activities were:
- more complex working conditions and aggravating factors and risks, both in the environment and in the constitution of the company

---

[1] https://appsso.eurostat.ec.europa.eu/nui/show.do?dataset=rd_e_berdsize&lang=en
[2] http://www.gim.com.mk/
[3] https://ec.europa.eu/commission/presscorner/detail/en/qanda_20_1150

- the trend of encouraging development, research and innovation, as the main drivers of development in the modern global economy and the main strategic commitment of the European Union
- rapid technological development, rapid obsolescence of technologies and technological skills, the need for long-term planning to upgrade knowledge, which will have a longer use value
- competitiveness in the market, based on modern ways of corporate organization, planning, management, operations and marketing
- phase of the life cycle in which the company is - reaching full maturity, which imposes the need to pursue goals and directions that will continue the upward trend of development, and will avoid stagnation and decline
- the company's tendency to expand more intensively on foreign markets

The company's vision is supported by constantly upgraded knowledge and innovation, applied for continuous improvement of services and participation in modern trends in science, technology and economy. Such a vision implies the development of the company not only as an important business actor in the economy, especially in the construction sector in the country and the region, but also in the direction of: application of the latest knowledge and technological achievements in operation, in accordance with national and European trends for sustainable development, use of many years of experience and knowledge in the service of the progress of science, economy and society.

Several aspects were observed before starting to build an innovative model for transformation toward achieving sustainable performance and KM and IC:
- Stage of the life cycle - the need to continue the trend of an upward line of development, and prevent stagnation and decline;
- Complex operating conditions and risks;
- Rapid technological development; and
- Necessity for long-term planning, upgrading the knowledge and organisational memory.

In the period of 2014-2020 a number of strategic decisions, innovative actions, structural measures, and organisational changes have been developed and implemented, based on the adopted strategies for investment and development of the IC in CEIM.

One of the first steps towards building a learning organisation was the establishment of an Advisory Body in CEIM, responsible for expansion of the international cooperation of CEIM, human capital development, preparation of infrastructure and scientific research projects, as well as utilization of funds from EU programs and funds.
CEIM made a decision to invest in science, i.e. research and development, as the highest achievement of social responsibility. Investing in science and development has a threefold impact. Above all, it encourages young people to further develop their research capacities, through the applicability of knowledge, then it directly affects the competitive advantage of CEIM, and finally this has a positive effect on the national economy of Republic of North Macedonia.

As a result of the cooperation and activities between the Board of Directors and the Advisory Board of CEIM, a new Private Scientific Institution "Institute for Research in Environment, Civil Engineering and Energy" (IECE)[4] was established in 2014, accredited by the Ministry of Education and Science.
Starting from 2014 several institutional projects for KM and IC were developed and implemented in CEIM, such as:
- The project "*Happy Employees, Successful Organisation*", which aimed to assess the human capital, focusing on their knowledge and propose initiatives to increase the human capital in CEIM. One of the initiatives was establishing internal Training centre.
- The project "*Rich Heritage, Powerful Future*", which focuses on activities, inspired by the rich heritage created over the past 45 years, proposing initiatives to manage IC and inspire innovative approach. One of the initiatives was establishing R&D centre.

CEIM's approach towards building a model for transformation and development of learning organisation, is reflected through their attitudes

---

[4] http://www.iege.edu.mk

toward the employees, enabling and nurturing work environment and organisational climate which ensures employees' engagement, motivation, and pursue for professional growth.

2. The infrastructure

In the process of building an innovative model for transformation and development of learning organisations towards sustainable performance, through KM and IC a large number of analyses were conducted to assess the current situation in CEIM, and then a series of measures and activities were developed and implemented in order to improve resources in each capital and successfully manage knowledge toward reaching the goal of becoming learning organisation.

A number of documents (strategies, rulebooks, manuals and guidelines) have been created and adopted, that serve as a basis and support for activities and support the transformation. All implemented activities are implemented in accordance with CEIM Strategies:
- Development strategy,
- Strategy for human resources management and
- Strategy for KM.

The summary of the strategic goals of these documents are presented in Table 1.

Table 1: CEIM Strategic documents and their objectives

Development strategy	Strategy for human resources management	Strategy for knowledge management
Building sustainable brand, maintaining reputation in the business and social spheres	Improving employee motivation and introducing new motivational techniques	Detection (mapping) of knowledge in CEIM (basic level, advanced level, specific knowledge, research potential)
Maintaining a competitive advantage in the domestic market	Performance management	
Expanding the operations in markets in other countries	Development of managerial and leadership skills of the Company's management staff	Lack or need for certain knowledge (training plan and professional development
Improving financial performance	Improving organisational culture	
Advancing existing services	Hiring experienced staff, experts in a specific field	Sharing, creating and retaining knowledge
Development of new services	Continuous development of staff	Organisational memory
Strengthening the capacities and nurturing the HR	Identification of competencies for each job position	Managing external knowledge networks and infrastructure
Continuity in investments	Talent management and career planning	

The most relevant strategic document for KM and IC is the KM strategy. The goal of the KM strategy is to create long-term value for CEIM by focusing on knowledge and building the necessary capacity to maintain its competitive advantage in the country and the region. Furthermore, the strategy supports maintaining the features of a learning organisation, adapting to the needs and challenges in its environment. The KM process is illustrated in Figure 1.

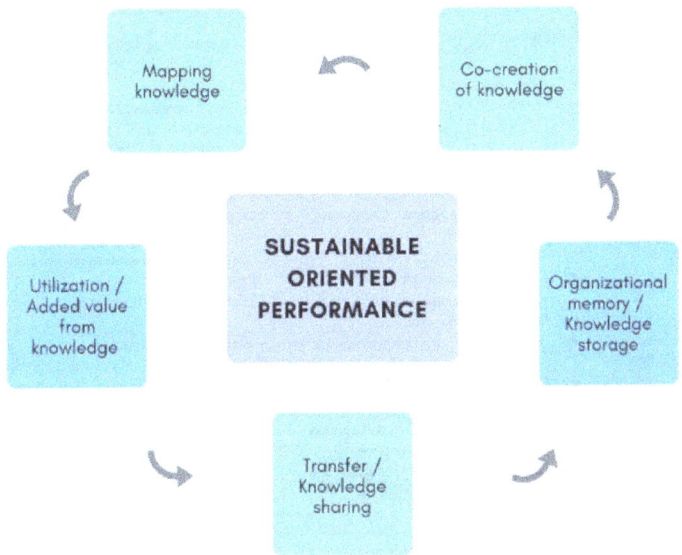

Figure 1: Process of KM in CEIM

In Table 2, an overview of the implemented activities for development of CEIM's IC is given. This table presents a complete picture of the process of management and measurement of IC and knowledge in CEIM, as well as insight into the investments made to encourage research, development, knowledge and growth of IC.

Table 2: Implemented activities for development of CEIM's IC

Type of capital	Actions (designed and implemented)	Indicators measuring progress
Human capital	• Knowledge management system • HR development program • Investments in education and trainings • Establishing internal Training center • Career development (assessment, plans) • Talent management • Performance management • Motivation techniques • Mentorship program	✓ Level of education ✓ Work experience and expertise ✓ Investments in human resource development (amount in euros, number of employees, number of trainings, etc.) ✓ Motivational techniques employed (material and nonmaterial) ✓ Level of career progress ✓ Number of mentors/mentees ✓ Employee engagement ✓ Risk in managing human capital
Structural capital	• Internal system for communication and data management • Employee Reward and Recognition Systems • New organisational structure and new managing job positions • Stimulating positive change in the organisational clime (team spirit, collaboration, unity)	✓ Investments in technology ✓ Changes in the organisational structure ✓ Number of new/upgraded products, services and process ✓ Number of new ideas, procedures, company standards ✓ Organisational structure/climate assessment ✓ Cooperation with academia ✓ Number of joint ventures
Relational capital	• Marketing and PR strategy • Re-branding activities • Market analysis of the region • Event management • New website • Building long term relations with clients	✓ Client satisfaction and loyalty ✓ Number/percentage of increased services, clients/returning customers ✓ Perception of company brand/image ✓ Promotional activities (social media, events, networks) ✓ Channels of communication and barriers
Innovation capital	• R&D Center • Investments in science • Model for co-creation of knowledge • Open model of innovation • Joint research projects • Industrial master thesis • Digital library • Internship program and supporting students	✓ Investments in research, development and innovation ✓ Number of joint research projects ✓ Number of research/educational projects funded by third party ✓ Number of conferences attended, papers published ✓ Number of new partnership with universities ✓ Number of MSc and PhD students from the employees
Process capital	• Strategy for growth • HR strategy • Knowledge management strategy • Code of conduct • Rulebook on HR education/trainings • Guidelines for competencies and career development	✓ New business model ✓ Unique approach ✓ Number and quality of new procedures/strategies/standards/guidelines ✓ Upgrades in the process of work methodology

In this context several activities are specially selected and emphasized because of their uniqueness and innovative aspect.

3. Human capital activities

CEIM is a large company, employing more than 300 people. Figures regarding the human resources of CEIM are presented in Table 3.

Table 3: Human resources of CEIM

Description	Category	Number of employees	Percentage of employees
Total number of employees		305	100%
Profile / Job positions	Managerial staff	32	10,49%
	Engineering staff	130	42,62%
	Technical staff	44	14,42%
	Operating staff	51	16,73%
	Administrative staff	48	15,74%
Gender structure	Men	211	69,18%
	Women	94	30,81%
Educational structure of employees	Bachelor level	122	40%
	Master level	42	13,7%
	PhD	1	0,32%
	Secondary education	101	33,11%
	Primary education	39	12,78%
Age structure	20-29 years	62	20,3%
	30-39 years	85	27,8%
	40-49 years	60	19,6%
	50-59 years	73	24%
	60-67 years	25	8,3%
Work experience	Up to 5 years	47	15,5%
	6 - 10 years work experience	52	17,0%
	11 - 15 years work experience	60	19,7%
	16 - 20 years work experience	32	10,5%
	21 - 25 years work experience	30	9,8%
	More than 25 years work experience	84	27,5%

Figure 2 shows the various aspects of human capital management. These aspects are important in creating a learning organisation that successfully adapts to changes in the environment and invests in its human capital.

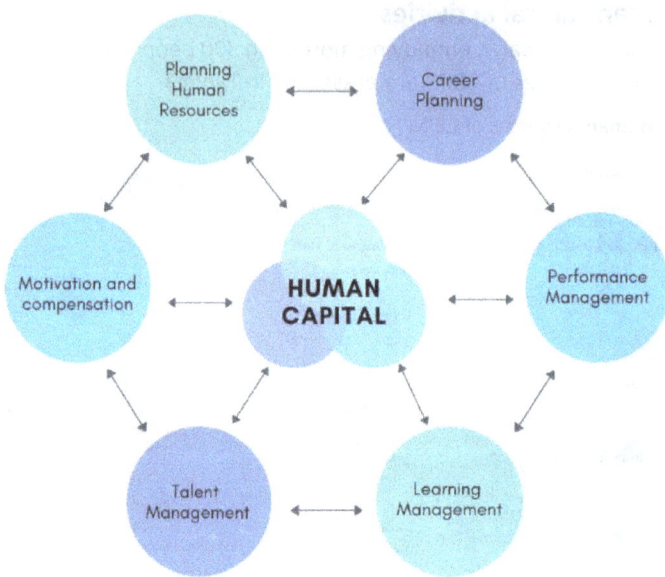

Figure 2: Human capital in CEIM

In each of the aspects of human capital, CEIM developed and implemented number of activities, as well as indicators to measure and evaluate the progress and effects.

Some of unique activities is establishing Training Centre in the company, recruitment of mentors and trainers, providing support for them through the Train the trainers program, jointly developing and implementing adult educational programs with academic institutions.

Also, a pool of talent employees was selected, and a special Professional program developed for them. CEIM started having annual learning plans, based on the assessed needs and industry trends. In the last 5 years, 296 employees have attended 103 different types of training. Part of these trainings are specialised educational programs lasting from 3 to 9 months, where CEIM actively participated in their development as co-creator, some are EU funded by the Erasmus + program, and part are funded by CEIM (around 30,000 euros).

4. Process capital activities

The **CO-IN model** (collaborative innovation partnerships) is a creation of the work of IECE and the way of functioning with CEIM. This model is based on mutual trust, creating community and synergy by applying a holistic approach.

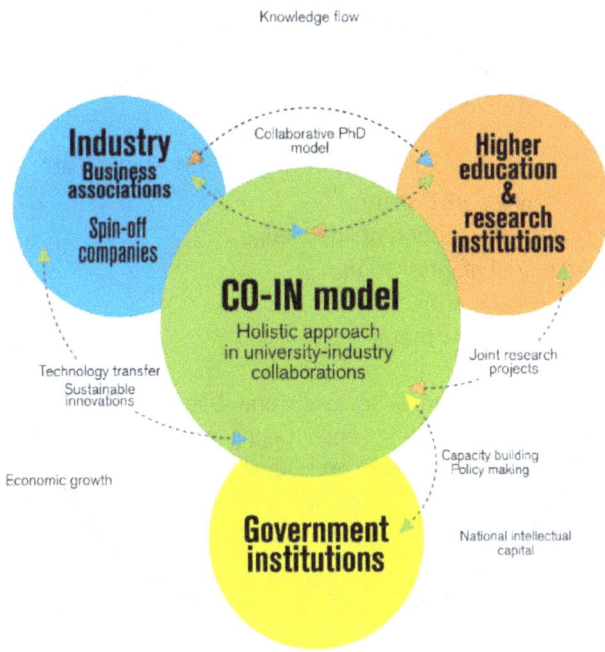

Figure 3: CO-IN model

The CO-IN model as unique model for enhancing competitiveness of companies and achieving sustainable growth of all participating organisations. It brings together the expertise and experience of sustainable innovation capability with new thinking and creativity from partners, creating

new business models in which ideas flourish. The CO-IN[5] model has been validated by the European Commission, which co-funded an Erasmus+ project: All4R&D[6], aiming to accelerate research, innovation, knowledge and technology transfer through enhancing strategic academia-industry alliances.
Innovation capital activities

In 2014 CEIM established the Institute for Research in Environment, Civil Engineering and Energy[7] (IECE). The institute is set to be a link between the academic and business community, and all programs and activities are oriented toward sustainability. IECE's mission is to increase the research and innovation potential of human capital in order to achieve added value and competitive advantage in the institutions with which it cooperates through collaborative partnerships. [8]

Specific activities developed jointly between CEIM and IECE are:
- Establishing a R&D Centre[9]
- Model for co-creation of knowledge
- Open model of innovation
- Joint research projects
- Industrial master thesis

In 2016 CEIM established a Research and Development Centre with the general objective of initiating, encouraging and coordinate the planning, organization, implementation and evaluation of the research and development activities of the company. The Centre is a functional link between CEIM and IECE in research, innovation and education projects.

The Centre provides for special type of services in the following fields:

---

[5]https://www.researchgate.net/publication/342698920_CO-IN_Model_as_a_holistic_approach_in_university-industry_collaboration_in_developing_countries
[6] https://all4rd.net/
[7] iege.edu.mk
[8]https://www.researchgate.net/publication/283451299_ENHANCING_COMPETITIVENESS_TROUGH_COLLABORATIVE_INNOVATION_PARTNERSHIP_-_A_CASE_STUDY_OF_MACEDONIAN_COMPANY
[9] http://www.gim.com.mk/?page_id=5166&lang=en

- strategic consultancy for development, research and innovation projects,
- development and actualization of research and innovation projects financed by national and international funds in collaboration with academic and scientific and research institutions, as well as other development centres in industrial companies,
- commercialisation of the research and innovation being implemented in the company, either independently or in collaboration with other institutions.

5. The challenges

Building an innovative model for transformation and development of learning organisation is far from easy and smooth. One important notion is that this is a long-term process and the benefits from it can be observed after few years. Very positive in this experience is the visionary leadership of the owners and the Supervisory board. Their support was crucial in addressing the challenges and overcoming them.

As previously mentioned CEIM and IECE established collaborative innovation partnership. One challenge was working in interdisciplinary teams. "Speaking the same language" meant creating mutual understanding, despite the different organizational settings and culture. Setting up teams with employees from partner institutions, rewarding collaborative activities and entrepreneurial mindsets was proven to be very positive in maintaining the partnership. This challenge was overcome with the approach *"Alone we can do little, together we can do so much more!"*

Other challenges that were observed are:
- Mindset of employees and managerial staff;
- Lack of time due to bad planning, too many obligations, motivation of managerial staff;
- The intangible aspect of the process;
- Change resistance – willingness to preserve old habits, structures, etc.

The challenges were addressed accordingly and vigorously. The most effective and efficient way to tackle them was through education. Different forms of acquiring new competences were used: one of one coaching, learning by doing, informal learning and training programs.

Having in mind the management staff in CEIM are mostly engineers, who never had formal education in management, and the topics of IC and KM were unfamiliar, special focus was put on their education. The managerial staff participated in 3 specialized programs for management and leadership:
- Engineering Management and Leadership Skills[10],
- Developing Marketing Solutions for Sustainable Brands, and
- Sustainability Leadership.

Also, in order to overcome the challenges and create positive clime for the transformation toward learning organisation, many other activities were implemented:
- Series of interviews with all employees were conducted;
- Upgrading risk management strategies;
- Improving time management skills of employees;
- Investing more time in planning resources and projects;
- 360° process for performance management and career development;
- Idea management system – initiatives to Propose an idea and Share knowledge;
- Material and nonmaterial incentives for higher motivation;
- Events for creating positive organisational climate, with focus on collaboration and sharing.

6. How the initiative was received by the users or participants

The collaboration established between CEIM and IECE is crucial in the success of all transformational processes. This form of "collaborative innovation" between a young organisation and an established company is recognized as valuable approach to innovation by the WEF.[11]

---

[10] http://mls4eng.iege.edu.mk/
[11] http://www3.weforum.org/docs/WEF_Collaborative_Innovation_report_2015.pdf

Figure 4: Collaborative innovation relation between CEIM and IECE

This partnership provides sharing complementary resources, combining efforts to support innovative ideas and creates significant value for both parties.

One successful practice is the Mentoring program, which includes 63 mentors. The program for is created from the need to nurture and transfer the knowledge of older employees to younger employees in CEIM.

Another positive feedback was received from the selected talented employees, who were willing to learn more and grow professionally, share knowledge, participate in joint research projects, become trainers, etc.

Also, very positive comments and great satisfaction was observed by CEIM clients and partners, who communicated their impressions of healthy and stimulating organisational climate and distinctive organisational culture, which added more value and affirmation of the benefits of the whole transformational process.

7. The learning outcomes

Monitoring the progress of KM and IC in CEIM and measuring effects and benefits from this transformation process is done with several quantitative and qualitative methods.

The VAIC model, proposed by Pulic was used for the quantitative calculation of IC. The VAIC model was used for the quantitative calculation of IC. The data for calculating the model was obtained from the financial statements of CEIM from the following years: 2013, 2015, 2017 and 2019.

For calculating IC with the VAIC model, the following variables are needed: human capital efficiency coefficient (HCE) structural capital efficiency coefficient (SCE) and capital employed efficiency coefficient (CEE).

Table 4: VAIC coefficient in CEIM

2013	2015	2017	2019
VAIC = 2,528373	VAIC = 2,8476	VAIC = 2,919465	VAIC=3,1307

The use of the VAIC model gives insight into how much new value is created per invested monetary unit invested in each resource, uncovering the overall efficiency of the organisation. A high coefficient shows a high level of value from the available portfolio of resources. VAIC above 2,50 is sign of very successful business results. This implies high level of efficiency, which leads to sustainable-oriented performance.

If we take into account the obtained coefficient according to the VAIC model, it can be concluded that in 2013 it was 2,53. There is an increase in the coefficient in 2015, when the coefficient is 2,85. In 2017, the VAIC coefficient was even higher at 2,92 and in 2019 the measured VAIC is 3,13.

One imperative for any organisation is that as important as it is to track value creation, it is vital to take care of the efficiency of the resources used in the business. In doing so, the relationship between the value added created and the IC (human and structural) is crucial. The research conducted and the results obtained for the measurement of CEIM's IC indicate the positive effects of the investments made in the last seven years in the company for development of research, knowledge and IC.

A qualitative and non-financial method was used to assess the IC of CEIM by using the Scandia model as a methodology. The questionnaire, consisting 123 statements consisted the following sections:
- **Human Capital** - Learning and education, Experience and expertise and innovation management;
- **Structural Capital** - Systems & programs and R&D;
- **Relational Capital** - Strategic alliances, licensing & agreements, Customer & Supplier relations and Customer Knowledge.

The results from the survey conducted with the questionnaire for IC in 2012 and 2019 are presented in Table 5.

Table 5: Average scores, difference and growth rate of the elements of IC in CEIM

Elements of intellectual capital		2012	2019	Difference 2019-2012	Growth rate
Human capital	Learning and education	3,42	3,97	0,55	16,08%
	Experience and expertise	3,35	3,69	0,34	10,15%
	Innovation and creation	2,83	3,23	0,40	14,13%
	Total	3,20	3,63	0,43	13,44%
Structural capital	Systems and programs	3,21	3,9	0,69	21,50%
	Research and development	2,84	3,7	0,86	30,28%
	Intellectual Property Rights	2,96	3,42	0,46	15,54%
	Total	3,003	3,67	0,667	22,21%
Relational capital	Strategic partnerships, licensing and agreements	3,15	3,81	0,66	20,95%
	Brand Organisation and Customer Relationship and Suppliers	3,25	3,98	0,73	22,46%
	Knowing the clients and associates	3,16	3,65	0,49	15,51%
	Total	3,19	3,81	0,62	19,44%

The results obtained during the measurement of IC show that there is an increase in the scores given for all types of IC between 2012 and 2019. The growth rate indicates a positive effect obtained from the investments made in the last seven years in CEIM and the perception of the management team about the achieved results.

The highest scores in 2012 were attributed to the following components of IC:

- Learning and education,
- Experience and expertise,
- Brand Organisation and Customer Relationship and Suppliers

In 2019 the highest scores were attributed to the following components of IC:
- Brand Organisation and Customer Relationship and Suppliers
- Learning and education,
- Systems and programs.

There is also an increase in the scores given to all types of IC from 2012 to 2019. The biggest differences calculated in the following components of IC are:
- Research and development,
- Brand Organisation and Customer Relationship and Suppliers,
- Systems and programs.
- Strategic partnerships, licensing and agreements
- Learning and education.

The growth of the scores in the research and development component clearly indicates the effects of investments in research, development and innovation in CEIM.

In table 6 selection of the most significant statements of human capital are presented, based on their relation to sustainability-oriented performance in CEIM.

Table 6: Average scores, difference and growth rate of the elements of human capital in CEIM

Learning and education	2012	2019	Difference 2019-2012	Growth rate
Employee development is crucial for the survival of the organisation.	4,0	4,5	0,5	12,50
The level of staff with higher education is on average in comparison with the industry (number of PhD, masters and graduates).	3,1	3,6	0,5	16,13
The organisation devotes a lot of time and effort to upgrading and developing the knowledge and skills of its employees.	2,9	4,0	1,1	37,93
The organisation manages the knowledge of employees.	3,0	3,6	0,6	20,00
Employee education affects the profitability of the organisation.	3,7	4,0	0,3	8,11
Experience and expertise	**2012**	**2019**	**Difference 2019-2012**	**Growth rate**
The organisation's employees are experts in their fields.	3,1	3,5	0,4	12,90
The organisation's employees are constantly giving the best of themselves, which makes this organisation different from others in the industry.	3,1	3,6	0,5	16,13
The abandonment of some employees of the organisation will cause problems in the work.	2,9	3,1	0,2	6,90
For employees with specific knowledge, the organisation has specific motivation measures.	2,9	3,5	0,6	20,69
The experience and expertise of the employees affects the profitability of the organisation.	3,9	4,3	0,4	10,26
Innovation and creation	**2012**	**2019**	**Difference 2019-2012**	**Growth rate**
The organisation has established a system of proposing new ideas.	2,3	2,8	0,5	21,74
A number of new products and services are made in comparison with competitors.	2,9	3,3	0,4	13,79
The organisation's employees are constantly encouraged to bring new knowledge and ideas and share their knowledge with colleagues.	3,0	3,8	0,8	26,67
There is a base of scientific and professional papers and literature available to the staff.	2,9	3,5	0,6	20,69
Creation and innovation by employees affect the organisation's market value (share value).	3,1	3,5	0,4	12,90

From the obtained results, it can be seen that there is a difference between the given scores for the conditions of the human capital in 2012 and 2019. The increase in the average scores for each statement is evident in all three groups: learning and education, experience and expertise, and innovation and creation.

Taking in consideration all activities implemented in CEIM, we can conclude that effects and benefits from KM and IC are multiple:
- the company's knowledge is properly stored, visible, used, and has an added value,
- new knowledge is co-created in joint research projects with Universities with applied focus relevant to the business strategy of the company,
- knowledge is shared with the mentorship and internship program,
- investments in IC positively influence the achievement of its business goals,
- organisational services and processes are upgraded or renewed, and
- the productivity and the organisational performance is improved and sustainability-oriented.

The advantages and benefits which emerged from the process of KM and IC towards sustainability-oriented performance have positive impact on all relevant stakeholders: meaningful jobs and career prospects for the employees, navigating the company towards achieving its vision for the managers, and higher return on their investments for the shareholders.

8. Plans to further develop the initiative

The last 5 years were of great importance for the future development of CEIM. Now, the navigation of the company will continue in continuously implementing the practices in KM and IC. Several new projects and initiatives are already started, focusing on relational capital and marketing solutions for sustainable brand.

Additional activities are foreseen in managing innovation capital, knowledge creation and transfer, as well as promoting and confirming the role of CEIM in research, education and innovation EU projects (funded by Horizon Europe and Erasmus + programs).

The experience of the Macedonian company CEIM and its transformation, the effects and benefits obtained are of great importance for developing countries and industry. The positive effect for other companies is that the developed and implemented actions for KM and IC can be replicated and further used by other organisation, motivated to enhance their development and sustainability-oriented performance. This transformation model from traditional to learning organisation, proposes a set of actions and measures, has innovative approach to follow the progress, using quantitative and qualitative methods. Additionally, the investments in knowledge and IC are directly linked to increasing the potential of human capital and the competitive advantage of the organisation.

The implications of the findings presented in this case are important from a practical perspective, as the information can assist managers to recognize the relevance of the topic and its importance, and support organisation development toward sustainability-oriented performance.

This case also provides practical implications in several areas such as discussion on the subject, new approaches in KM, implementation of proactive initiatives in IC, mitigating sustainability risks, creating and implementing strategies on sustainable development, and promoting awareness on the importance of sustainable business practices.

This Macedonian company serves as an inspiration and role model for other companies in developing countries to follow this example, replicate, and benefit from KM and IC. The Factory Karpos[12], which is a large company in the construction industry with more than 70 years of experience, is in the initial phase to start the transformation process toward learning organisation.

The analysis indicates that employees in developing countries, value the knowledge as an important asset of their operations and at the same time recognize that companies make certain attempts towards creating and emphasizing the value of knowledge. Although both employees and organisations see the value and importance of knowledge, still major instruments related to knowledge, KM, organisational learning and talent management are not in place or a scarce in developing countries. One of the main focus points for organisations should be creating a stronger climate committed towards knowledge creation. At the same time incentives and programs for supporting KM should be introduced, which will dramatically

---

[12] https://mk.fabrikakarpos.com.mk/

change the path of development of companies in developing countries and their economy in total.

This case study has a wider impact on society level as well, contributing to building knowledge-based economy, economic growth and development in developing countries. The knowledge-based economy places great importance on the diffusion and use of information and knowledge as well as its creation through developing knowledge networks. The determinants of success of enterprises, and of national economies as a whole, is ever more reliant upon their effectiveness in gathering and utilizing knowledge This impact can be strengthened and long lasting, if government, professional bodies and associations support this process of managing knowledge and IC on micro level and create incentives for companies who work in a sustainable manner.

Author Biographies

Ass. Prof. Slavica Trajkovska, PhD in Labour Economics, is the founder of IECE, private research institute, positioned to be an interface between industry and academia. She has 25 years of experience working in management and leadership positions. Slavica is a professor and consultant in KM, Intellectual capital, Sustainable organisations and brands.

Prof. Dr. Angelina Taneva-Veshoska, PhD in Management, is the Director of IECE. Her research and teaching interests include Intellectual Capital, Sustainability, Organizational Behavior, R&D, HRM, CSR and Ethics. She has 17 years of experience developing and implementing educational programs, international projects and capacity building activities.

Srecko Trajkovski is an entrepreneur and a visionary leader, owner of the Civil Engineering Institute MACEDONIA JSD Skopje. He has extensive experience of more than 30 years in management and leadership positions. He strongly supports investments in knowledge, R&D&I and intellectual capital.

www.ingramcontent.com/pod-product-compliance
Lightning Source LLC
Chambersburg PA
CBHW071332190426
43193CB00041B/1759